Warrior Athletes

by
Robert Bigart
and
Joseph McDonald

Warrior Athletes:

Some Salish and Kootenai Indian Sports Stars

by
Robert Bigart
and
Joseph McDonald

published by
Salish Kootenai College Press
Pablo, Montana

distributed by
University of Nebraska Press
Lincoln, Nebraska

2022

Cover illustrations: Left: Nick Lassa in Oorang Indian football out-
fit, 1922-1923. Courtesy Marion County Historical Society, Marion, Ohio.
Right: Marvin Camel. Courtesy Renee Camel, Pablo, Montana.
Cover design by Corwin Clairmont, graphic artist, Ronan, Montana.

Library of Congress Cataloging-in-Publication Data:
Names: Bigart, Robert, author. | McDonald, Joseph, 1933- author.
Title: Warrior athletes : some Salish and Kootenai Indian sports stars / by
    Robert Bigart and Joseph McDonald.
Other titles: Some Salish and Kootenai Indian sports stars.
Description: Pablo, Montana : Salish Kootenai College Press, 2022. | Includes
    bibliographical references and index. | Summary: "The story of some promi-
    nent twentieth century Salish and Kootenai athletes from the Flathead Indi-
    an Reservation in western Montana. Includes Charles Allard, Jr.: University
    of Montana Grizzly football star, 1898-1901; Two Feathers, William Matt,
    and Henry Matt: wrestlers, 1903-1905; Nick Lassa: Kalispel Indian Foot-
    ball Star, 1911-1923; Jimmy Dupuis: Flathead Reservation fistic warrior,
    1930-1940; Frenchy Roullier and Sam Clairmont: Ronan athletic stars,
    1925-1940; Archie McDonald: Haskell Institute and Montana Grizzly
    football star, 1930-1939; and Marvin Camel: Native American two time
    world boxing champion, 1962-1990"--Provided by publisher.
Identifiers: LCCN 2022031157 | ISBN 9781934594339 (paperback)
Subjects: LCSH: Indian athletes--Montana, Western--Biography. | Salish In-
    dians--Montana, Western--Biography. | Kootenai Indians--Montana, West-
    ern, Biography. | LCGFT: Biographies.
Classification: LCC E99.S2 B547 2022 | DDC 305.897/07860922--dc23/
    eng/20220816
LC record available at https://lccn.loc.gov/2022031157

published by
Salish Kootenai College Press
PO Box 70, Pablo, MT 59855
Distributed by
University of Nebraska Press,
1225 L Street, Suite 200, Lincoln, NE 68588-0630,
order 1-800-848-6224, www.nebraskapress.unl.edu.

Table of Contents

Introduction, by Joe McDonald   1

Chapter 1
Charles Allard, Jr: University of Montana
    Grizzly Football Star, 1898-1901   5

Chapter 2
Two Feathers, William Matt, and Henry Matt:
    Wrestlers, 1903-1905   15

Chapter 3
Nick Lassa: Kalispel Indian Football Star, 1911-1923   29

Chapter 4
Jimmy Dupuis: Flathead Reservation Fistic Warrior,
    1930-1940   45

Chapter 5
Frenchy Roullier and Sam Clairmont: Ronan Athletic
    Stars, 1925-1940   53

Chapter 6
Archie McDonald: Haskell Institute and Montana
    Grizzly Football Star, 1930-1939   73

Chapter 7
Marvin Camel: Native American Two-Time World
    Boxing Champion, 1962-1990   89

Index   101

Introduction

Stories of Outstanding Athletes of the Flathead Indian Reservation

Throughout the years of American Indian history, the Indians participated in competitive sports competition, sports that were indigenous to their lifestyle. They had footraces, knife throwing, and archery contests. They had horse races and gambled on the results. When reservation life started, the competitive games changed. The sports became baseball, boxing, wrestling, football, and basketball.

There have been so many tribal member athletes over the years it was difficult to decide who to include in this book. The athletes chosen were those that the authors could find information about. The information came from newspaper articles, interviews, high school and college annuals, and family keepsakes. The book is limited to tribal member athletes who competed from 1900 to World War II. The exception being Marvin Camel the tribes' world champion boxer.

As a tribal member growing up on the Flathead Indian Reservation and loving sports, I heard many stories from elders about the athletic prowess of certain individuals. I listened intently as the stories were told of some of the athletic feats of our tribal people. We could find no written record of the athletic accomplishments of many of those we heard stories about. We limited the athletes we wrote about to those who we could find written records about their success in competitive athletic contests.

As our reservation was being settled by homesteaders, beginning in 1910, public schools were slow to develop and so were sports programs. Some Indian families attended the rural public schools and there were no athletic programs to participate in. Many of our young tribal members were sent away to distant boarding schools, and there they could participate in athletic programs and be on teams representing those schools. The schools that had well known sports programs were Carlisle and Haskell and they were a long way from the Flathead Indian Reservation, being located in Pennsylvania and Kansas.

Some of our people were outstanding athletes at these schools, but the news seldom got to the reservation. We only heard about their athletic accomplishments in handed down oral stories told by family members and sports enthusiasts. Carlisle played major colleges in football and other sports. Basketball was just beginning its evolution into being a major sport. Jim Thorpe, a Sac and Fox tribal member, started his famous career there. A little later in the 1900s Haskell became a major player in the sports world.

Locally on the reservation, wrestling got a great deal of attention and later boxing. Matches were held in Charlo, Ronan, and Polson. Outstanding wrestlers and boxers had matches in Missoula, Spokane, and other cities in the northwest. Travel was usually by train. The newspapers would give day to day accounts of when the featured wrestler or boxer arrived in Missoula or Spokane and their day to day training was reported to an enthusiastic reader audience. The matches were reported in the paper round by round or fall by fall.

The federal government encouraged sports participation as a way to spur Indian people to join the mainstream of the general population of the United States. It did this locally and in the boarding schools. The Indian people responded by participating in the sports that were available. Baseball became popular and it was easy to build a diamond in a field with a backstop. The sport became popular right away for men in the local communities. Small communities had teams that played in leagues. Dixon, Camas Prairie, Charlo, Moiese, and others had competitive teams. The older Archie McDonald and his brother James (Bugs) were very well-known players. They played on different teams. Archie was a pitcher and pitched in Missoula leagues. We could not find any writeups on his games, only box scores. Later his cousin Archie McDonald became a well-known football player, playing at Haskell, the University of Montana, and professional teams. World War II ended his football career. This book is to refresh some people's memories about the athletic accomplishments of some our early athletes and help those interested learn about these great athletes.

When our Indian people went to the boarding schools in the early days, they were placed in school according to their reading levels and other academic skills. Some were placed in grade school some in high school, and some in post high school trade programs. They were all eligible to play for the schools' teams. My dad attended Haskell and played football. He told about his friend, who was married, had children, and was in the fourth grade, and played on Haskell's football team. Archie McDonald was in high school at Haskell and played on the football team. His Haskell team played Notre Dame and he played the entire sixty minutes of the game. Some great players evolved from this time at the boarding schools. The most notable was Nick Lassa from Camas Prairie. He played at Carlisle and later played professional football under the direction of team manager Jim Thorpe.

As public schools developed and small gyms were constructed, basketball and track became popular sports. The gyms were small, backboards were constructed out of wood, there was a center jump after each basket, and the fans crowded the sidelines. Basketball games were played in the winter. There was great community interest in these games. The Ronan High School Tornadoes became the Ronan Chiefs during this early era of basketball.

There are so many stories to be written about the athletic exploits of some of our tribal members. It would be wonderful for all of us if families would take time and write about their members who excelled in sports. These stories could be put together in a book and they would be preserved forever.

We hope that you enjoy reading about these athletes. They brought a great deal of pride to their families and to the Confederated Salish and Kootenai Tribes. This book was made possible by the research of Bob Bigart. He studied old newspapers that he found in archives, on library microfilm, and old school papers where the athletes attended. In one case he had to buy the microfilm in order to get access to the information he was searching for. He visited with relatives of some of the athletes that played in the late 1920s and early 1930s. In the Marvin Camel story, he was able to visit with his brothers and sisters. We owe Bob a big thanks for his work.

Joe McDonald

Chapter 1

Charles Allard, Jr.: University of Montana Grizzly Football Star, 1898-1901

A Flathead Reservation tribal member was a Grizzly football star at the Montana State University in Missoula at the turn of the twentieth century. Charles Allard, Jr., was a member of the 1898 and 1900 Grizzly teams and captain in 1901. Allard had attended college at Gunnery Military Academy in Washington, Connecticut, and the College of Montana at Deer Lodge before his enrollment at the Montana State University in Missoula in February 1898.[1]

In October 1898, the university football team took up a collection among the student body and raised $110 to pay for coaching, travel, and equipment expenses.[2] Allard returned to the university in October 1898 and missed the first part of the football season. He did make it back on the team in time to take part in a 0 to 18 loss to the Anaconda Athletic Club on October 29, 1898. He played the right halfback position.[3]

The Grizzlies beat the Bozeman State College team twice in November 1898. Allard was not listed in the starting lineup for the November 12 game played at Bozeman. Bozeman lost this game 0 to 6.[4] The second contest was played on Thanksgiving Day, November 24 at Missoula. Allard played the fullback position and, according to the *Daily Missoulian*, "was loudly cheered" when he kicked the first field goal in the state of Montana. According to the *Anaconda Standard* reporter, "Allard's play at full back was splendid." The Grizzilies won the second game 16 to 0.[5]

The final game of the 1898 season was played against the Helena Athletic Club. This game was aborted after 20 minutes of play when the Helena team disputed a call by the umpire. The Helena team stormed off the field when the Grizzlies were ahead by 6 to 0.[6]

Allard and most of the rest of the 1898 Grizzly football team were not in school and did not play on the 1899 team. The 1899 team beat the Anaconda Athletic Club team and had two games with the Montana State College. The Grizzlies lost both games with the Bozeman school.[7]

By the fall of 1900, Allard was back at the university and had rejoined the Grizzly football team as a halfback. The team practiced regularly through November, but efforts to arrange games were unsuccessful except for the Thanksgiving contest with the Bozeman college.[8]

On November 6, 1900, a "Ladies' Football society" was formed by the university women students. The society was to cheer on the team and care for "the wounded when any of the gentlemen members of the football team are injured during practice or in a regular game."[9] During the 1900 season George Taylor broke his leg and George Ferrell suffered from a broken collar bone during Grizzly practices.[10] The student newspaper editorialized that "Our football team is a practical example of 'the survival of the fittest,' from a physical standpoint. He whose bones are least susceptible to breaks, is the one who stands the best show to remain on the team. Our invalids are all convalescing."[11]

Allard played one of the starring roles in the Grizzlies' loss to Bozeman on Thanksgiving, November 29, 1900: 11 to 12. Allard scored one of the Grizzlies' two touchdowns in the second half. According to the *Missoulian* reporter, Allard "made a touchdown on as pretty a play as could be asked for. . . . The work of Allard was another strong feature of the home boys' game."[12] The Grizzly coach, Frank Bean, wrote that "Allard played a star game, and without his help we would have been seriously handicapped. His previous experience enabled him to help me materially in coaching."[13] An unnamed *Kaimin* writer observed, "Allard can play football, and he can make a touchdown in spite of bulky, husky hayseeds."[14]

Top: Charles Allard, Jr.,
University of Montana Grizzly Football Captain, 1901.
Detail from UM87-0020, Toole Archives, Mansfield Library,
University of Montana, Missoula.
Bottom: Charles Allard, Jr., in later life.
Detail from June Allard Green and Joe Green, *Joseph Allard,*
1876-1964 (n.p., 1986), p. 77.

Allard returned to the university on October 16, 1901, with his friend and teammate Oscar Sedman. Allard was captain of the 1901 Grizzlies and played halfback.[15] He joined the team just before they played in Missoula against an all Indian team from the Fort Shaw Indian School on October 19, 1901. Allard was kept out of that game by "a slight injury during practice on Friday. Allard was determined to play at any cost, and it was with difficulty he could be kept on the side lines." The Grizzlies suffered a humiliating 0 to 5 loss to the Indian team.[16] According to one report, "The Fort Shaw game was a disagreeable spectacle of roughness."[17]

A week later on October 26, 1901, the Grizzly team lost their second game of the season played against the Butte High School football team in Butte, 11 to 25. At one critical point, "Allard attempted to punt out for Missoula, but fumbled." Despite that failure, the *Anaconda Standard* reported that "Allard played a good kicking game."[18]

The pride of the Grizzlies was somewhat salved by two victories over the team of Fort Missoula soldiers. The Grizzlies won the November 2, 1901, game by 12 to 0 and the November 9, 1901, encounter 26 to 0. Allard played a prominent role in both victories: "Allard has, from the start, in spite of being handicapped by several injuries of a more or less serious nature, played his usual phenomenal game. To his cool headed and clever work as captain much of the excellent work of the team is due." In the second Fort Missoula game, Allard ran 50 yards for one touchdown and 45 yards for another.[19]

In between the two games against Fort Missoula, on November 8, 1901, the Grizzlies played the Butte Business College in Missoula.[20] On November 20, 1901, the Grizzlies won a rowdy game against the Ben West Colts 26 to 6. The Colts were a team of local Missoula players. Brawls broke out between supporters of each team and even among the players. Allard made several goal kicks, made a 20-yard gain in one play, and did "magnificent work."[21]

The climax of the 1901 Grizzly season was the November 28, 1901, contest in Bozeman against the agricultural college team. The Grizzlies lost the game 0 to 31. Allard played right halfback and made gains of five to ten yards. He played "a star game," but, according to the *Missoulian*, could not compensate for the "listless" performance of his teammates.[22]

On January 23, 1902, a theatrical play, "The Octoroon," was performed as a fund raiser for the Athletic Association at the university. According to one report, it raised $100 to help with travel and equipment expenses for the football team.[23]

* * * * * * * * * *

Allard's football career ended in 1901, but he went on to raising cattle, organizing rodeos, racing horses, and playing a prominent role in Flathead Reservation politics. He never graduated from Montana State University.[24]

Charles Allard, Jr., was born on October 26, 1878, the second son of Louis Charles Allard, Sr., and Emerence Brown Allard.[25] Charles, Sr., was famous on the reservation as a rancher raising cattle and buffalo and the operator of an early stage line through the reservation.

In June 1902, the younger Allard organized the Great Buffalo and Wild West Show featuring buffalo from his family herd and Indian performers hired on the Flathead Reservation. The show was a cooperative venture with several Missoula white entrepreneurs including a Mr. Hutchin. The show played in Missoula and Anaconda before embarking on a Midwest tour. The show encountered bad weather in the Midwest and went broke that fall in Marshalltown, Iowa. In 1906, Allard won the interstate relay horse race at Spokane and also competed in that event at the western Montana fair in Missoula.[26]

In later years, Allard promoted stampedes or rodeos in Missoula and other Montana cities. He was one of the directors of the Missoula Stampede over the Fourth of July 1917. Along with horse races and trick ropers, the stampede featured Jackson

Sundown, a famous Nez Perce Indian rodeo performer. A number of Indians from the Flathead Reservation found employment at the celebrations.[27]

Allard invested in a number of business ventures on the Flathead Reservation in the early twentieth century. In 1903, Allard and his football buddy, Oscar Sedman, owned the Polson trading post formerly operated by Henry Therriault. Allard started a stage line across the reservation in 1909. In 1909 and 1910, he invested in two newly established banks in Polson.[28]

But there were some bumps in the road. On January 11, 1907, Benjamin H. Denison, a former trader on the reservation, complained to the Indian Rights Association in Philadelphia that Allard was "heavily indebted to and looks after many interests of Missoula Merc[antile] Co."[29] In December 1918, Allard and his wife were sued over an overdue promissory note owed to the First National Bank of Ronan.[30]

Allard was active in tribal politics. In 1910, a general council of tribal members chose him to be on a delegation to Washington, D.C., to discuss tribal affairs with officials there. In the 1910s, he was secretary of the Flathead Business Committee which supported Agent Fred C. Morgan's policies which led to loss of considerable Indian owned land on the reservation. Duncan McDonald was chairman of the Business Committee. It was opposed by the Flathead Tribal Council that wanted a total revision of agency policies on the reservation.[31]

Charles Allard, Jr., died at his home on the reservation June 26, 1930. He was buried at St. Ignatius.[32]

Endnotes

1. *Daily Missoulian*, Dec. 14, 1897, p. 8, c. 2; "Charles Allard Dead," *The Montana Record-Herald* (Helena, Mont.), June 28, 1930, p. 11, c. 1; June Allard Green and Joe Green, *Joseph Allard, 1876-1964: Pioneer, Cowboy, Stagecoach Driver, Rancher* (n.p., 1986), p. 3; "At the University," *Daily Missoulian,* Feb. 16, 1898, p. 1, c. 2, and p. 2, c. 2.

2. "Getting Down to Work," *The Anaconda Standard*, Oct. 9, 1898, p. 14, c. 2-3.

3. "Football Tomorrow," *Daily Missoulian*, Oct. 28, 1898, p. 8, c. 2; "Students Meet Defeat," *The Anaconda Standard*, Oct. 30, 1898, p. 5, c. 1.

4. "Bozeman vs Varsity." *The Kaimin* (University of Montana, Missoula), Nov. 1898, p. 16; *Daily Missoulian*, Nov. 8, 1898, p. 8, c. 1; Bob Gilluly, *The Grizzly Gridiron* (Missoula: Montana State University Press, 1960), p. 61.

5. "Missoula Notes," *The Anaconda Standard*, Nov. 19, 1898, p. 12, c. 1; "The Football Game," *The Anaconda Standard*, Nov. 22, 1898, p. 12, c. 3; Gilluly, *The Grizzly Gridiron*, pp. 61-62; "It Was a Hot Contest," *The Anaconda Standard*, Nov. 25, 1898, p. 12, c. 2; "Thanksgiving Kicks," *Daily Missoulian*, Nov. 25, 1898, p. 1, c. 4.

6. "It Was a Raw Outfit," *The Anaconda Standard*, Dec. 4, 1898, p. 18, c. 2; *Daily Missoulian*, Dec. 5, 1898, p. 8, c. 3.

7. Gilluly, *The Grizzly Gridiron*, pp. 62-63; "Bozeman, 6; Missoula, 0," *The Missoulian* (weekly), Nov. 17, 1899, p. 1, c. 5.

8. "Anaconda Backed Out," *The Anaconda Standard*, Nov. 19, 1900, p. 10, c. 2; "A Magnificent Game Won by Bozeman at Missoula," *The Anaconda Standard*, Nov. 30, 1900, p 1, c. 1-2.

9. "Ladies' Football Society," *The Anaconda Standard*, Nov. 7, 1900, p. 12, c. 3.

10. "Had His Leg Broken," *The Missoulian* (daily), Nov. 24, 1900, p. 4, c. 1-2; "Broken Collar Bone," *Edward's Fruit Grower & Farmer* (Missoula, Mont.), Nov. 30, 1900, p. 5, c. 4.

11. *The Kaimin*, Nov. 1900, p. 5.

12. "Bozeman 12 Missoula 11," *The Missoulian* (daily), Nov. 30, 1900, p. 1, c. 3-4; "A Magnificent Game Won by Bozeman at Missoula," *The Anaconda Standard*, Nov. 30, 1900, p. 1, c. 1-2.

13. Frank Lamoreaux Bean, "Review of the Football Season of 1900 at U. of M.," *The Kaimin*, Dec. 1900, pp. 9-10.

14. "Locals," *The Kaimin*, Dec. 1900, p. 15.

15. "Old Players Back," *The Missoulian* (daily), Oct. 17, 1901, p. 5, c. 3; "Fort Shaw Team Wins," *The Anaconda Standard*, Oct. 20, 1901, p. 13, c. 2-3.

16. "Varsity Loses Football Game," *The Missoulian* (daily), Oct. 20, 1901, p. 1, c. 1-2, and p. 4, c. 5.

17. "Didn't Like the Rough Work," *The Anaconda Standard*, Nov. 4, 1901, p. 10, c. 3.

18. "Just Like a Steam Plow," *The Anaconda Standard*, Oct. 27, 1901, p. 9, c. 4.

19. "'Varsity Makes Winning Score," *The Missoulian* (daily), Nov. 3, 1901, p. 1, c. 1-2; "Football," *The Kaimin*, Nov. 1901, pp. 11-12; "Second Game with Fort Missoula," *The Kaimin*, Nov. 1901, p. 12.

20. "Missoula Notes," *The Anaconda Standard*, Nov. 5, 1901, p. 12, c. 4.

21. "University Beats Colts," *The Anaconda Standard*, Nov. 21, 1901, p. 14, c. 2; "Varsity Team Defeats Colts," *The Missoulian* (daily), Nov. 21, 1901, p. 1, c. 3, and p. 5, c. 5.

22. "Boys Anxious to Win," *The Anaconda Standard*, Nov. 26, 1901, p. 14, c. 4; "Both Missoula Teams Defeated," *The Missoulian* (daily), Nov. 29, 1901, p. 1, c. 4-5; "College 31, University 0," *The Anaconda Standard*, Nov. 29, 1901, p. 11, c. 4-5.

23. "Editorials," *The Kaimin*, Jan. 1902, pp. 5-6; Gilluly, *The Grizzly Gridiron*, p. 64.

24. Maria Mangold, Registrar, University of Montana, Missoula, to Bigart, Oct. 4, 2021, email.

25. "Louis Charles Allard, Sr.," Eugene Mark Felsman, Confederated Salish and Kootenai Tribes family group sheets, McNickle Library, Salish Kootenai College, Pablo, Mont.

26. Robert Bigart and Joseph McDonald, eds., *The Indians Were Prosperous: Documents of Salish, Pend d'Oreille, and Kootenai Indian History, 1900-1906* (Pablo, Mont.: Salish Kootenai College Press, 2021), pp. 98-100 and 338-39.

27. Robert Bigart and Joseph McDonald, eds., *"We Want Freedom and Citizenship": Documents of Salish, Pend d'Oreille, and Kootenai Indian History, 1912-1920* (Pablo, Mont.: Salish Kootenai College Press, 2021), pp. 242-44.

28. Bigart and McDonald, eds., *The Indians Were Prosperous*, pp. 74-78; Robert Bigart and Joseph McDonald, eds., *"Us Indians Don't Want Our Reservation Opened": Documents of Salish, Pend d'Oreille, and Kootenai Indian History, 1907-1911* (Pablo, Mont.: Salish Kootenai College Press, 2021), pp. 194-97 and 238-39.

29. B. H. Denison, Missoula, Mont., to M. K. Sniffin, Indian Rights Association, Philadelphia, Penna., Jan. 11, 1907, incoming correspondence, reel 19, Indian Rights Association Papers, 1864-1968.

30. Bigart and McDonald, eds., *"We Want Freedom and Citizenship,"* p. 297.

31. Bigart and McDonald, eds., *"Us Indians Don't Want Our Reservation Opened,"* pp. 249-55 and 259-61; Bigart and McDonald, eds., *"We Want Freedom and Citizenship,"* pp. 131-33 and 219-21.

32. "Charles Allard Dead," *The Montana Record-Herald* (Helena, Mont.), June 28, 1930, p. 11, c. 1; "Charles Allard Funeral Is Held at St. Ignatius," *The Ronan Pioneer*, July 3, 1930, p. 1, c. 6.

Chapter 2
Two Feathers, William Matt, and Henry Matt: Wrestlers 1903-1905

Three Flathead Reservation tribal members wrestled professionally in Montana and surrounding states between 1903 and 1905: Abel "Two Feathers" Gravelle and William and Henry Matt. Two Feathers, a Kootenai Indian, wrestled white opponents in Washington, Montana, British Columbia, Minnesota, and Ohio. There was no official body dispensing titles, but in a December 1904 advertisement he was billed as the "Champion Indian Wrestler of the World."[1] In 1903 a white wrestler from Kalispell, Montana, named Jack O'Neill took charge as Two Feather's trainer and manager. Newspaper accounts describe Two Feathers as six feet and four and a half inches tall and weighing 215 pounds. A 1904 newspaper article claimed he was 23 years old, but Flathead Agency records indicate he was born in 1877 and was 27 years old in 1904.[2]

Two Feathers' parents were Francois Gravelle from Savoy, a European kingdom that later was divided between France and Italy, and Isabelle, a Kootenai Indian woman. His granduncle, Kootenai Chief Eneas Big Knife, had been 6 feet 4 inches tall.[3] In 1889, his parents operated a restaurant and hotel for travelers near the Kootenai village on Flathead Lake.[4]

Two Feathers' first wrestling contest was against Frank A. Gotch in December 1903 and apparently took place in Whatcom, Washington. Two Feathers was thrown by Gotch in this match.[5]

A couple of months later, on March 7, 1904, Two Feathers lost another wrestling match against the American, Duncan

McMillan. This contest took place in Victoria, British Columbia. Two Feathers won two falls but failed to secure a third fall in time to win the match.[6] Two weeks later on March 21, 1904, Two Feathers won a match held at Tacoma, Washington, against Chris Person, a Tacoma wrestler. Two Feathers secured two falls in succession. The winner earned the side bet of $100 and 75 percent of the gate receipts.[7] Two days later on March 23, 1904, Two Feathers lost a rematch with Frank Gotch at Vancouver, British Columbia. Gotch got two straight falls. The winner got more than $1,200.[8]

Two Feathers wrestled both Chris Person of Tacoma and John Berg of Bellingham at Tacoma, Washington, on March 30, 1904. Two Feathers threw Berg twice and Person once to secure three out of five falls from his two opponents.[9]

On April 13, 1904, Two Feathers got a rematch with Duncan McMillan who had beaten him on March 7, 1904, in Victoria. Two Feathers got three falls on McMillan in ninety minutes to take the victory. Two Feathers' manager, Jack O'Neill of Kalispell, wrestled John Berg of Bellingham. Berg was the winner of his match getting two out of three falls.[10]

Two Feathers had another match with John Berg and Chris Person in Seattle later in April 1904. Two Feathers had agreed to throw the two opponents four times in 90 minutes. He threw Person twice and Berg once, but he failed to throw Berg a second time. As it turned out, Berg threw Two Feathers once by the end of the match.[11]

On December 21, 1904, Two Feathers had a rematch with Duncan McMillan in Spokane. Two Feathers agreed to throw McMillan three times in an hour. On his way to Spokane, Two Feathers walked 55 miles from his home on the reservation to the Northern Pacific Railroad where he caught the train to Spokane. Before the match, Two Feathers appeared in Indian clothes on the streets of Spokane: "As he is six feet five inches tall in moccasins and dresses in hand woven blankets covered with weasel and ermine skins, he makes a striking figure." The winner got 60 percent of the ticket revenue. Unfortunately, Two Feathers was

"Two Feathers, Chief of the Kootenais,"
The Kalispell Bee, July 5, 1907, page 1, col. 3-4.
Courtesy of Northwest Montana Historical Society,
Kalispell, Montana.

Event Extraordinary
GREAT
4 WRESTLING 4
MATCHES
AUDITORIUM--SPOKANE
WEDNESDAY EVENING **Dec. 21**
CHIEF
TWO-FEATHERS
Champion Indian wrestler of the world, vs.

D. A. McMILLAN
Champion Mixed Wrestler.

CONDITIONS OF MATCH—Indian to throw McMillan three falls in one hour, catch-as-catch-can style, for purse of $300. Match will be preceded by three good preliminaries.

Prices 50c, 75c .and $1.00. Stage Seats $1.50.

Tickets on sale at box office, Monday, December 19.

TROUBLE AT 8:30

Ladies can attend as well as gentlemen.

"Event Extraordinary," *Spokane Press*, Dec. 21, 1904, p. 3, c. 5.

unable to throw McMillan three times in an hour and McMillan won the match.[12]

Two Feathers' next opponent was a Cuban, Clarence Bouldin, in Cleveland, Ohio, in early January 1905 in front of a crowd of 1,200 spectators. Two Feathers was thrown twice by Bouldin and lost the match.[13]

On February 18, 1905, Two Feathers lost a rematch with Frank Gotch in St. Paul, Minnesota. Gotch agreed to throw Two Feathers and Jim McAuley, a St. Paul wrestler, two times each in an hour. This time Gotch won the match. Two Feathers' manager Jack O'Neill met Captain Whitmore in a preliminary bout.[14]

To keep up the intensive schedule, Two Feathers met Carl Mattson, the local Minneapolis champion, on March 2, 1905, in Minneapolis, Minnesota. Jack O'Neill also appeared in a preliminary bout.[15]

Only a few weeks later, on March 22, 1905, 800 people watched Duncan McMillan throw Two Feathers at Spokane. McMillan won three out of five rounds. The winner got three fourths of the gate receipts. Newspaper reports credited Two Feathers with superior quickness and skill, but McMillan showed better technique. As part of the entertainment, Two Feathers' manager, Jack O'Neill, threw seven amateur wrestlers in less than an hour.[16]

Two Feathers was scheduled to wrestle Ole Marsh in Spokane on April 5, 1905, but at the last minute Two Feathers did not show up. No reason was given for his absence, but the newspapers soon carried a bizarre report that Two Feathers had been killed in a saloon row by Ben Cramer, a white man married to a Flathead tribal member. The rumored murder did not occur, and Two Feathers was alive and well on the reservation and working for Angus McDonald, a reservation rancher.[17]

The match with Ole Marsh was rescheduled for May 5, 1905, in Spokane. The purse for the winner was $250 and the gate receipts. An audience of 600 people witnessed Ole Marsh throw Two Feathers for three falls out of four in the Spokane Theater. The newspaper reported that, "At times both would throw science to the winds and match strength and speed. As in his other matches at Spokane, the Indian was a marvel at quick recovery, and struggled on the defensive most of the time. Marsh was the aggressor, leading the struggle all the way." On the same bill, Jack O'Neill threw four amateur wrestlers in less than an hour. [18]

Two Feathers' next match was with Duncan McMillan in Missoula on May 12, 1905. Two Feathers went into training in Missoula and made several public appearances to publicize the fight:

> Two Feathers has been the object of much cu-
> riosity since he arrived here [in Missoula] and
> his massive form dressed in beaded buckskins,
> makes a striking appearance on the streets. Those
> who have seen the big Indian wrestler state that
> his style of wrestling will be revelation to many
> and is distinctively his own. His long arms and
> legs enable him to put into execution many new
> holds which baffle his opponents.

A few days before the match, Two Feathers attended a cantata, "Queen Esther," at the Missoula opera house.[19] Missoula newspapers noted several Flathead Reservation residents who came to Missoula for Two Feathers' bout: Mose Grenier; William V. Bell, Jr.; and Henry Matt, also a wrestler.[20]

On May 12, 1905, Two Feathers won the match with Duncan McMillan by taking two falls out of three. McMillan won the first fall, but Two Feathers took the last two. In another fight on the card, Two Feathers' manager, Jack O'Neill, knocked out Jack Curran.[21]

Two Feathers' last known professional wrestling bout was on May 26, 1905, against Jack Curran of Missoula. Two Feathers' fight followed a contest between Jack O'Neill of Kalispell, and William Matt of Arlee. Two Feathers had agreed to throw Jack Curran four falls in an hour. He secured only two falls and lost the match.[22]

Henry Matt in wrestling outfit.
Courtesy Virginia Matt Brazill, Arlee, Montana.

UNION OPERA HOUSE

A. H. HARTLEY, Manager • MISSOULA, MONTANA

THURSDAY, JUNE 8
GRAND HANDICAP

Wrestling Match

William Matt vs. Jack Curran
Jack O'Neill vs. Big Henry Matt
And Three Others

Seats on Sale Wednesday at 4 p. m.

Prices, 50c., 75c., $1   **Stage Seats $1.50**

"Union Opera House,"
The Daily Missoulian, May 23, 1905, page 6, col. 6-7.

Abel "Two Feathers" Gravelle apparently retired from wrestling after May 1905. He had married a Kootenai woman named Cecille in 1900 and died on October 27, 1935.[23]

William and Henry Matt, Wrestlers

Two other Flathead Reservation tribal members wrestled for money in 1905. Henry and his cousin, Will Matt, were descendants of a French and Blackfeet family that had been adopted into the Bitterroot Salish tribe in the nineteenth century. Henry Matt was born in Stevensville, Montana, in 1872. His cousin, William Matt, was born on the reservation in Arlee in 1885. The first newspaper article on the Matt family wrestlers claimed Henry had attended Carlisle Indian School in Pennsylvania and mastered wrestling and other sports as a student.[24]

Henry did attend Carlisle briefly in 1893 and 1894 when he was 21 years old. But he was only there for less than five months. According to the surviving Carlisle student records, Henry arrived at the school on November 28, 1893, and he ran away with two other Montana Indian students on April 27, 1894. The other two deserters were Ashbury Blodgett from Flathead and John Sanborn, a Gros Ventre. It is hard to believe that Henry's abbreviated Carlisle schooling provided much time to develop his wrestling skills. No record was found of William attending Carlisle.[25]

No matter what his background was, on April 11, 1905, Henry Matt was in Missoula to arrange a match between his cousin, William, and Jack Curran, a Missoula wrestler.[26] On April 12, 1905, the Matts made a deal for Jack Curran to meet William later that month.[27]

When the match occurred, on April 21, 1905, Will Matt beat Jack Curran. Curran threw Will once, but Curran was thrown three times. According to the newspaper, several hundred dollars was wagered on the fight and "the Matt family of the reservation covered all of the money as fast as it came in sight." In the preliminary bout that evening, Duncan McMillan threw Henry Matt twice in twenty minutes of wrestling. Some of Jack

Curran's supporters started a rumor that Will Matt was a professional wrestler passing himself off as a Flathead Reservation cowboy. Will was defended by the local newspaper.[28]

Will Matt's next bout was on May 26, 1905, in Missoula with Jack O'Neill, the Kalispell wrestler and manager for Two Feathers. O'Neill had a fifteen-pound advantage over Will, but Will won the match with three out of five falls.[29]

On June 3, 1905, Will and Henry Matt gave a wrestling exhibition in Plains, Montana. Will offered to throw any five local men in one hour or forfeit $25. Will won the first, third, and fourth falls and then entertained the spectators by bending 60-penny spikes into staples with "scarcely any effort."[30]

Will and Henry Matt's wrestling career seemed to come to an end after a match on June 8, 1905, in Missoula. Will had agreed to throw Jack Curran four times within an hour. Will got only two rounds before Curran threw him in the third round. According to the local newspaper, Will had a number of side bets on the match and as a result was a considerable loser. On the same card, Jack O'Neill promised to throw Henry Matt five times in an hour. O'Neill won four rounds, but Henry won the fifth round and therefore the match.[31]

There was some talk of a rematch between Will Matt and Jack Curran, but nothing seemed to come of it.[32] Will went on to marry Margaret St. Mark, a Chippewa-Cree woman, in 1913, and he died in Polson on June 7, 1970.[33]

Henry Matt, however, went on to a long and prominent role in tribal affairs. He was often called on to serve as interpreter for Indians in the state courts and for tribal chiefs negotiating with white men.[34] He was long a thorn in the side of the Flathead Agents, particularly Fred Morgan who was agent and superintendent between 1908 and 1917.

Henry was frequently charged with selling bootleg alcohol on the reservation.[35] He encouraged tribal members to fight the Flathead Agency policy of micromanaging the affairs and money of tribal members.[36] In 1911 and 1912, Henry, his brother Alexander, and Chief Martin Charlo were active in organizing

Flathead Reservation chapters of the Brotherhood of North American Indians. The Brotherhood was a national organization working to reduce federal government control of tribal affairs.[37]

Henry was also a well-known fiddler on the reservation. He married Marguerite Pokerjim on August 22, 1896, and the family had thirteen children. He died on October 5, 1956, at St. Ignatius, Montana.[38]

Conclusion

Two Feathers Gravelle had a several year career in wrestling and defeated a number of white opponents. In 1905, William and Henry Matt had a short sprint wrestling in Missoula, Montana. The Matts both won and lost some very interesting matches that involved considerable gambling income and cost. The wrestlers were an important part of the cultural mosaic of local sports in early twentieth century western Montana.

Endnotes

1. "Event Extraordinary," *The Spokane Press*, Dec. 20, 1904, p. 3, c. 5.

2. "Jack O'Neil in Canada," *Flathead Herald-Journal* (Kalispell, Mont.), Jan. 7, 1904, p. 6, c. 3-4; "Abel 'Two Feathers' Gravelle," Eugene Mark Felsman, Confederated Salish and Kootenai Tribes family group sheets, McNickle Library, Salish Kootenai College, Pablo, Mont.

3. "Abel 'Two Feathers' Gravelle," Eugene Mark Felsman, Confederated Salish and Kootenai Tribes family group sheets, McNickle Library, Salish Kootenai College, Pablo, Mont.; Rev. James O'Connor, "The Flathead Indians," *Records of the American Catholic Historical Society of Philadelphia*, vol. 3 (1888-91), p. 104.

4. Robert J. Bigart, *Providing for the People: Economic Change Among the Salish and Kootenai Indians, 1875-1910* (Norman: University of Oklahoma Press, 2020), p. 126.

5. "'Two Feathers' to Meet M'Millan," *The Daily Missoulian*, Nov. 21, 1904, p. 8, c. 2; "Jack O'Neil in Canada," *Flathead Herald-Journal* (Kalispell, Mont.), Jan. 7, 1904, p. 6, c. 3-4.

6. "'Two Feathers,' Lost the Match," *The Seattle Star*, Mar. 8, 1904, Night edition, p. 5, c. 4.

7. "Two Feathers Bests Person," *The Tacoma Times*, Mar. 22, 1904, p. 3, c. 1.

8. "Gotch Won the Match," *The Seattle Star*, Mar. 24, 1904, p. 7, c. 4.

9. "Chief Two Feathers Is a Wonder," *The Tacoma Times*, Mar. 31, 1904, p. 4, c. 3-4.

10. "Wrestling Match Was a Hippodrome Affairs," *The Seattle Star*, Apr. 14, 1904, p. 2, c. 2-3; "Red Wins, Jack Loses," *The Kalispell Bee*, Apr. 19, 1904, p. 8, c. 1.

11. "Indian Failed," *The Seattle Times*, Apr. 28, 1904, p. 2, c. 4.

12. William B. Goode, "World of Sport," *The Spokane Press*, Dec. 14, 1904, p. 2, c. 3-4; "Chief Two Feathers to Meet M'Millan," *The Daily Missoulian*, Dec. 19, 1904, p. 9, c. 4; William B. Goode, "World of Sport," *The Spokane Press*, Dec. 22, 1904, p. 2, c. 3-4; William B. Goode, "World of Sport," *The Spokane Press*, Dec. 28, 1904, p. 2, c. 3-5.

13. "Two Feathers Goes Twice to Mat," *The Daily Missoulian*, Jan. 13, 1905, p. 2, c. 1.

14. "Gotch Gets Away with Mat Artists," *The Saint Paul Globe*, Feb. 19. 1905, p. 30, c. 1.

15. "Chief to Wrestle in Minneapolis," *The Saint Paul Globe*, Mar. 2, 1905, p. 5, c. 3.

16. "M'Millan Throws Two Feathers," *The Spokesman-Review* (Spokane, Wash.), Mar. 23, 1905, p. 3, c. 1; William B. Goode, "The Popular Sports," *The Spokane Press*, Mar. 23, 1905, p. 2, c. 3-4.

17. "Spokane Theatre," *The Spokane Press*, Apr. 3, 1905, p. 2, c. 7; William B. Goode, "The Popular Sports," *The Spokane Press*, Apr. 6, 1905, p. 21, c. 3-6; "Two Feathers May Be Dead," *The Kalispell Bee*, Apr. 7, 1905, p. 1, c. 3; "Two Feather Is Alive," *The Anaconda Standard*, Apr. 12, 1905, p. 12, c. 4.

18. "Two Feathers to Wrestle," *The Daily Missoulian*, Apr. 29, 1905, p. 6, c. 1; "Marsh Throws the Indian," *The Spokesman-Review*, May 6, 1905, p. 3, c. 4.

19. "Two Feathers Goes in Training," *The Daily Missoulian*, May 8, 1905, p. 6, c. 5; "Two Feathers in Training," *The Anaconda Standard*, May 9, 1905, p. 12, c. 5; "Big Indian Admired," *The Anaconda Standard*, May 11, 1905, p. 12, c. 5-6.

20. *The Daily Missoulian*, May 13, 1905, p. 6, c. 3-4 (three items).

21. "Two Feathers Wins Match with M'Millan," *The Anaconda Standard*, May 13, 1905, p. 14, c. 3; "Two Feathers Wins Wrestling Bout," *The Daily Missoulian*, May 13, 1905, p. 5, c. 2.

22. "Union Opera House," *The Daily Missoulian*, May 23, 1905, p. 6, c. 6-7; "Matt Bests Jack O'Neill," *The Anaconda Standard*, May 27, 1905, p. 14, c. 6.

23. "Abel 'Two Feathers' Gravelle," Eugene Mark Felsman, Confederated Salish and Kootenai Tribes family group sheets, McNickle Library, Salish Kootenai College, Pablo, Mont.

24. "Henry Matt" and "William Matt," Eugene Mark Felsman, Confederated Salish and Kootenai Tribes family group sheets, McNickle Library, Salish Kootenai College, Pablo, Mont.; *The Missoula Journal*, Apr. 4, 1905, p. 3, c. 1.

25. Henry Matt Student Information Card, Records of the Carlisle Indian Industrial School, RG 75, National Archives, series 1329, box 13; Register of Pupils – Discharged, 1890-1909, Records of the Carlisle Indian Industrial School, RG 75, National Archives, series 1324, p. 157.

26. Henry Matt, "Ready to Wrestle," *The Daily Missoulian*, Apr. 11, 1905, p. 8 c. 4.

27. "Curran Matched to Wrestle with Indian," *The Anaconda Standard*, Apr. 13, 1905, p. 12, c. 1-2.

28. "Will Matt Defeats Jack Curran," *The Daily Missoulian*, Apr. 22, 1905, p. 8, c. 2-3; "Will Matt Leaves for North," *The Daily Missoulian*, Apr. 23, 1905, p. 2, c. 1; "Fair and Square," *The Daily Missoulian*, May 28, 1905, p. 10, c. 2.

29. "Union Opera House," *The Daily Missoulian*, May 23, 1905, p. 6, c. 6-7; "O'Neill Is Defeated by Wm. Matt," *The Daily Missoulian*, May 27, 1905, p. 8, c. 4.

30. *Plainsman*, June 2, 1905, p. 1, c. 1; "A Clever Wrestler," *Plainsman*, June 9, 1905, p. 1, c. 4.

31. "Curran Is Winner of Match," *The Daily Missoulian*, June 9, 1905, p. 8, c. 5; "Curran Wins from Matt," *The Kalispell Bee*, June 13, 1905, p. 3, c. 1.

32. "Wrestlers Talk of Match," *The Daily Missoulian*, June 10, 1905, p. 6, c. 2.

33. "William Matt Dies at Polson," *The Daily Missoulian*, June 9, 1970, p. 7. c. 3.

34. See for example Robert Bigart and Joseph McDonald, eds., *The Indians Were Prosperous: Documents of Salish, Pend d'Oreille, and Kootenai Indian History, 1900-1906* (Pablo, Mont.: Salish Kootenai College Press, 2021), pp. 170, 175, and 181; Robert Bigart and Joseph McDonald, eds., *"We Want Freedom and Citizenship": Documents of Salish, Pend d'Oreille, and Kootenai Indian History, 1912-1920* (Pablo, Mont.: Salish Kootenai College Press, 2021), p. 94.

35. See for example Robert Bigart and Joseph McDonald, eds., *"Us Indians Don't Want Our Reservation Opened": Documents of Salish, Pend d'Oreille, and Kootenai Indian History, 1907-1911* (Pablo, Mont.: Salish Kootenai College Press, 2021), pp. 188-90; Bigart and McDonald, eds., *"We Want Freedom and Citizenship,"* pp. 130, 172, and 193.

36. See for example Bigart and McDonald, eds., *"Us Indians Don't Want Our Reservation Opened,"* pp. 188-90; Bigart and McDonald, eds., *"We Want Freedom and Citizenship,"* pp. 134-38 and 181-86.

37. See for example Bigart and McDonald, eds., *"Us Indians Don't Want Our Reservation Opened,"* pp. 329-36; Bigart and McDonald, eds., *"We Want Freedom and Citizenship,"* p. 24.

38. "Henry Matt, 84, Taken by Death," *The Daily Missoulian*, Oct. 6, 1956, p. 7, c. 5; "Henry Matt," Eugene Mark Felsman, Confederated Salish and Kootenai Tribes family group sheets, McNickle Library, Salish Kootenai College, Pablo, Mont.

Chapter 3
Nick Lassa:
Kalispel Indian Football Star,
1911–1923

One of the most colorful Flathead Reservation athletes during the first half of the twentieth century was Nick Lassa. He was a descendent of Kalispel or Lower Pend d'Oreille Indians who had been relocated from eastern Washington to the Flathead Reservation during the late 1880s. Nick Lassa was born on July 11, 1898, to Lassaw and Mary Michell of Camas Prairie on the reservation. He had a younger sister named Louise Lassaw.[1]

Between about 1914 and 1918, Nick Lassa was a member of the Carlisle Indian Industrial School football team in Pennsylvania. He also excelled at track and as a debater and public speaker. Carlisle closed in 1918 and Lassa transferred to the Haskell Institute in Kansas. He played football and track for Haskell between 1918 and 1921. In 1922 and 1923, he was a member of the first, and only, all-Indian team in the National Football League. After the late 1920s, he returned to the Flathead Reservation where he married, raised a family, and was a prominent tribal councilman. The life of Nick Lassa, 1898-1964, was the legend of a remarkable tribal athlete and leader.

Carlisle Indian School Student, 1911–1918
In March 1911, Nick Lassa was one of the first twelve Indian students from the Flathead Reservation to enroll in the Carlisle Indian Industrial School in Carlisle, Pennsylvania. Lassa was twelve and a half years old at the time. The nine boys and three girls in the party traveled to Pennsylvania by rail and were escorted by H. S. Allen, the chief clerk at Flathead Agency.

According to Allen's account, when one of the students, Jim
Kallowat, became homesick for Flathead, Lassa

> was a sure cure for the blues, however, and it was
> only a few moments until Jim again was thinking
> of the distance to Carlisle instead of the many
> miles between himself and Flathead. . . . Nick,
> perhaps, was the liveliest of the party. Among the
> jokes perpetrated by the Indians, usually head-
> ed by Nick, was the drawing on an old, soiled
> handkerchief of a buffalo, a horse, etc., with a
> common lead pencil, and the sale to a young
> fellow in search of something "real Indian" for a
> quarter. The Indians also had a good laugh over
> Nick's story about being with Buffalo Bill and re-
> ceiving $5.00 per day for riding; that he was only
> going to Carlisle until the show started out in the
> spring. A small scar on his cheek, after he learned
> how the white people to whom he was talking
> were ready to believe and anxious to hear such
> stories, developed into a scar caused by being
> shot through the cheek with a rifle while engaged
> in a fight.[2]

According to the Carlisle school records, Lassa had attended the
St. Ignatius Mission boy's school for four years before coming to
Carlisle. He enrolled at Carlisle on March 2, 1911.[3]

Lassa was to remain at Carlisle for seven and a half years
until August 29, 1918, when he was twenty years old. Carlisle
was closed in 1918, and Lassa transferred to the Haskell Institute in Lawrence, Kansas. In the summers of 1913, 1914, 1915,
1917, and 1918, Lassa was placed with Eden V. West of Prince-
ton, N.J., as part of Carlisle's outing system. His trade at Carlisle
was listed as "painter," but his summer work in New Jersey was
likely agricultural.[4] In 1914, his trade course was listed as "shoe-
making."[5]

In September 1913, Lassa was elected captain of the newly
organized football team among the younger students.[6] Possibly

in the fall of 1914, but certainly by the fall of 1915, Lassa was on the famed Carlisle Indian football team. On October 23, 1915, he played left guard for the Carlisle team in a scoreless tie against a white team from Bucknell.[7] In November 1915, Lassa "was showered with congratulations from all sides for his wonderful playing in the West Virginia game. 'Lassa Back,' is the name of one of the latest Varsity plays."[8] His enthusiastic training was noted in the school newspaper: "Nick Lassa enjoys training so much that every evening after football practice he generally has a cross-country run by himself."[9]

In the fall of 1916 season, Lassa was listed as one of the coaches helping with the tryouts for the 1916 football team.[10] In 1917, Lassa played left guard when the Carlisle team defeated a team from Albright College 59 to 0.[11] Later that year, Lassa was praised by the *New York Sun*: "The only star over the Redskins tepee was Lassa, who played speedy, intelligent and altogether game contest at left tackle against Annapolis. He followed the ball like a hound and generally was to be found under the pile when a scrimmage was stopped."[12]

But Lassa excelled in other sports and academics at Carlisle. During the basketball season, Lassa was a cheerleader for the Carlisle team. In January 1915, he was "a very capable leader for the rooters." In February 1918, he and the other cheerleaders were "inspiring and helpful and had much to do with the fine spirit displayed."[13]

In the spring, Lassa excelled at track events. At a February 27, 1915, meet Lassa threw the sixteen-pound shot put 39 feet and six inches.[14] In February 1916, he competed in the short sprints and high jump.[15] In a March 28, 1917, meet, Lassa won the shot put (35 feet) and discus throw (90 feet). In June 1917 in the commencement week competition, Lassa won the discus throw, and placed second in the shot put and hammer throw.[16] In April 1918, Lassa placed second in the shot put in a competition with Lebanon Valley College. A month later in a meet with Gettysburg, he won first in the shot put (38 feet) and second in the hammer throw. In 1918, Lassa lettered in track for Carlisle.[17]

There are a few other references to other athletic sports. In January 1916, Lassa was training in wrestling. No further references were found documenting his wrestling activities.[18] Lassa was working out with weights in March 1917.[19] In January 1918, he was coaching an intermural basketball team at Carlisle.[20]

Lassa also participated in other aspects of student life at Carlisle. In March 1917, he presented an unnamed selection, possibly a speech, at a meeting of the Holy Name Society, the Catholic student association on campus. Lassa gave an extemporaneous speech at a Holy Name meeting in January 1918. Finally, he gave a talk at another meeting of the society in May 1918.[21]

In March 1916, Lassa was fifth corporal of troop D of the student military corps at Carlisle.[22] In November 1917, he donated $2 to the Carlisle chapter of the American Red Cross. He made a $5 special Christmas donation to the Red Cross in December 1917. Another $5 was donated to the Knights of Columbus War Camp Fund in March 1918.[23]

Lassa's biggest non-athletic efforts at Carlisle occurred through his membership in a debating society named the "Invincibles," which he joined in January 1916.[24] At the end of January 1916, he gave an extemporaneous speech and took part in his first debate. Lassa argued the affirmative that gravy had more nutrition than beans.[25] During the remainder of the 1915–1916 school year, Lassa gave two talks and argued the negative against the re-election of President Woodrow Wilson.[26]

In the 1916–1917 school year, Lassa expanded his role in the Invincibles. In November 1917, he served as a judge of a debate on whether Benjamin Franklin or Isaac Newton was the "greater man." He delivered an extemporaneous speech at a December 1916 meeting and was elected treasurer of the Invincibles in April 1917. At the April 27, 1917, meeting of the society, Lassa gave a declamation on "Spartacus to the Gladiators."[27]

During the next school year, 1917–1918, Lassa gave talks or treasurer reports at most meetings of the Invincible Debating Society. On October 1, 1917, Lassa, as the Invincibles' treasurer, delivered a donation of $5 to the local branch of the Red

Cross. At the December 7, 1917, meeting of the Invincibles, Lassa gave the students a preview of the speech he was to deliver at the Philadelphia meeting of the Indian Rights Association on December 14, 1917. At a March 1918 meeting the president of the debating society was absent and Lassa led the society song during the opening ceremony. At the last meeting of the society in April 1918, Lassa won a competitive speech contest and made his "usual snappy report."[28]

Lassa also gave various public speeches outside of the debating society. In November 1916, he gave a declamation on the start of World War I at a benefit for Armenian refugees in the Near East. As part of the American Indian Day celebration at Carlisle on May 12, 1917, Lassa spoke on "Red Jacket's Speech on White Man's Religion." Lassa gave a report on his December 14, 1917, speech to the Indian Rights Association. General Richard Henry Pratt, the Carlisle Superintendent, was in the Philadelphia audience. In April 1918, Lassa gave a patriotic speech and was awarded a certificate as one of the best speakers.[29]

In October 1916, Lassa was in the Carlisle hospital for several weeks for an unidentified illness. By October 28, 1916, he was out of the hospital and attending a football game.[30]

In 1918, the United States Congress closed Carlisle and Lassa and many of his classmates transferred to Haskell Institute in Lawrence, Kansas. Many Carlisle Indian students found the regimentation and cultural indoctrination to be repressive, but Lassa was able to find some positive experiences in his time there. He excelled in football and track, a campus debating society, and joined the Catholic student organization.

Haskell Institute, 1918–1921

Lassa played football at Haskell for four years from 1918 to 1921. He was a speaker at the June 1919 athletic banquet.[31] On September 27, 1919, he contributed to a blowout 71 to 0 win over the Kansas University of Commerce with a drop-kick from the 38-yard line.[32] Lassa played right guard during the December 1919, 7 to 0 defeat of the St. Xavier College team at Cincinnati,

Ohio.[33] On February 13, 1920, Lassa was one of the 19 Haskell football players to receive a football sweater for the 1919 season.[34]

Lassa was one of the speakers at a September 24, 1920, football rally at the start of the 1920 season.[35] He played left guard in Haskell's October 15, 1920, 33 to 6 victory over the Hays Normal football squad.[36] A couple of weeks later, on November 5, 1920, Haskell defeated Marquette University in Milwaukee 6 to 3. Lassa and the other linemen "displayed their usual fight."[37] Lassa gave a talk about his recent football trip to Cincinnati at the November 28, 1920, meeting of the Sacred Heart Society at Haskell.[38]

At the annual football banquet on December 1, 1920, Lassa was complimented for playing "splendid football." Lassa also spoke at the banquet about "Football When I Was a 'Little Feller.'" He announced

> that he never was little. He remembered, however, when he was several years younger than now and "swiped" his mother's apron, put leaves in it and tied it up to use as a football. Although a great eater, he declared he would rather play football than eat. Football, he considers, a great thing for the Indian and makes a good Indian out of him.[39]

According to the Haskell student newspaper, Lassa was "the largest man on the Haskell team. He weighs around 195 and, when in action, reminds one of a run-away truck."[40] Lassa received his letter in football at the June 7, 1921, athletic banquet at Haskell.[41]

Lassa's last season at Haskell was in 1921. He played left guard during Haskell's October 29, 1921, 21 to 0 victory over Tulsa University.[42] He also played on November 12, 1921, during Haskell's loss to Notre Dame 7 to 42.[43]

The shot put was Lassa's primary spring athletic event. On May 1, 1920, he placed third in competition with the College of Emporia.[44] During the 1921 season, Lassa competed in an inter-society track meet against other Haskell students. Lassa got third in the high jump, second in the shot put, and third in the discus.[45] Later that spring, on April 19, 1921, Lassa won the shot put competition with the Kansas Aggies. He threw the 16-pound shot 42 feet and 3 inches.[46] In an early May 1921 rematch with the Kansas Aggies, Lassa threw the shot put 39 feet 9 inches.[47]

The Sacred Heart Society was the Catholic student organization at Haskell. Lassa led a prayer to close the September 28, 1919, meeting of the society.[48] Lassa was one of the special guests at a Knights of Columbus banquet in Lawrence, Kansas, on May 21, 1920.[49] As mentioned before, Lassa gave a talk about a recent football trip to Cincinnati at the November 28, 1920, meeting of the society.[50] In 1921, Lassa was president of the Sacred Heart Society of Haskell Institute.[51]

Lassa also took part in the student military organization at Haskell. He had the rank of major and gave a talk at the November 13, 1920, officers' party.[52]

In June 1921, Lassa graduated from Haskell in masonry. He gave a talk at the graduation exercise on "The How and Why of Trade Training at Haskell." The speech outlined all the different training programs offered in trades.[53] In addition, Lassa played a Quitoan general and counsellor in an contemporary adaptation of an ancient Peruvian play, "Ollanta," presented on June 2, 1920.[54]

He was president of the 1921 Haskell vocational class and was elected president of the alumni association. At the class day program he urged the students "to continue in school and get a more thorough education."[55]

Oorang Indian, 1922–1923

Nick Lassa's love for football and his ties to Jim Thorpe provided the 1922 opportunity for Lassa to join the most remarkable team of the fledgling National Football League. Thorpe was a Sac and Fox Indian who had won a national reputation playing football for the Carlisle Indian Industrial School in Pennsylvania and winning major events in the 1912 Olympic Games in Stockholm, Sweden.

Nick Lassa in Oorang Indian football outfit, 1922-1923.
Courtesy Marion County Historical Society, Marion, Ohio.

In 1922, Thorpe teamed up with Walter Lingo, a white Ohio entrepreneur who had developed a thriving business breeding and selling airedale dogs. Thorpe was to assemble an all-Indian football team to play in the National Football League as the Oorang Indians. Their home base, LaRue, Ohio, did not even have a football field, but Lingo was most interested in using the team to promote his airedale dog business.

Lassa and the other Indian players entertained the audiences with pre-game and halftime shows. They exhibited the airedale dogs trailing and treeing game. The players also dressed up in Indian regalia and performed Indian dances, tomahawk throwing, and knife and lariat demonstrations. The team helped sell a lot of airedale dogs, but also became known for drinking and parties off the field. A Chicago bartender wanted to close early, but the Indian football players threw him into a telephone booth, turned it upside down, and continued to celebrate. They lost a game to the Chicago Bears after partying until dawn the night before the game. In the end, the Indians only won three games during the two seasons they played.[56]

Stories of Nick Lassa's physical prowess, friendship, and partying made him one of the most colorful Oorang Indian players. He stayed in Ohio for several years after the team was disbanded in 1923. His Indian name was "Long Time Sleep" which he earned because his teammates had trouble waking him up in the morning.

After 1923, Lassa found part-time work in the LaRue, Ohio, area and frequently wrestled carnival wrestlers and local competitors for money. When drinking, he frightened the women working nights at the local telephone office, but he was also remembered for acts of kindness. Bank robberies were common in the area in the early 1920s, and, when a local woman had to work alone in the bank at noon, Lassa came to her aid. He stayed in the bank and read the newspaper during noon hours.

One Sunday, Lassa and two of his teammates, Jim Thorpe and Pete Calac, helped a local farmer castrate some boars which weighed about 350 pounds each. The three jumped into the smelly pen and threw the pigs by hand. When they were done, they climbed a water tank to wash off. Afterwards, they sunned on the tank, drying off in the nude.

Local sheriffs and judges told stories about Lassa's troubles while drinking. One time a local white man complained Lassa was drunk and threatening him with a butcher knife. When the mayor showed up to settle matters, Lassa gave the mayor the knife and said, "I was just waitin' for someone to come and get it."

One young LaRue resident, Bob Greenwood, remembered Lassa jumping into a freezing river to help chop the ice to free a trapped boat. Lassa asked Greenwood for help getting out of the water but ended up pulling Greenwood into the freezing water. Other times, Lassa would ask Greenwood to run to a nearby town with him. When the boy tired, Lassa would lift him up to ride on his shoulders. Sometime in the late 1920s or early 1930s, Lassa left Ohio to return to the Flathead Reservation in Montana.[57]

Later Years, 1930–1964

Nick Lassa gave up alcohol and moved back to Camas Prairie on the Flathead Reservation in the late 1920s or early 1930s. On February 7, 1937, he married Rose Sorrell at St. Ignatius Mission. The couple had twin daughters in October 1937: Marie "Buzzie" Wheeler and Marian "Skee" Pichette. A son was born in 1946, Nick Lassaw, Jr. Nick and Rose also adopted Zella M. Lassaw, Nick's cousin born in 1955.

Nick served on the Confederated Salish and Kootenai Tribal Council between 1935 and 1939 and 1948 to 1951. In 1938, Nick resigned from the council because he had moved out of his old district. After a request from tribal members for him to remain on the council, he withdrew the resignation. Later in 1938, he was appointed chief of the tribal police.[58]

Nick worked at many different jobs over the years to support his family. He worked on the Kerr Dam construction, local sawmills, and even the mines in Idaho.

Nick Lassa,
Confederated Salish and Kootenai Tribes Tribal Council,
1935-1939 and 1948-1951.
Courtesy Confederated Salish and Kootenai Tribes, Tribal
Council, Pablo, Montana.

According to his daughter Buzzie, her father was nice but very strict. He laughed a lot and was a lot of fun. Nick was a legend at area powwows where he danced with a buffalo horn headdress. He was the whip man who frightened children who were not paying attention to the dancing.

He died at St. Patrick Hospital in Missoula on September 4, 1964. He left a number of grandchildren and a life of exuberance and adventure equaled by few others.[59]

Endnotes

1. "Lassaw," Eugene Mark Felsman, Confederated Salish and Kootenai Tribes family group sheets, McNickle Library, Salish Kootenai College, Pablo, Mont.

2. "Indian Students to Carlisle," *The Daily Missoulian*, Feb. 28, 1911, p. 10, c. 4; H. S. Allen, "Twelve Flathead Indian Students Have Enjoyable Journey to Carlisle," *The Daily Missoulian*, Mar. 26, 1911, ed. section, p. 1, c. 1-7, and p. 5, c. 4.

3. Nicholas Lassau Progress Card, Records of the Carlisle Indian Industrial School, series 1330, box 1, RG 75, National Archives, Washington, D.C.; Nicholas Lassau Student Information Card, Records of the Carlisle Indian Industrial School, Student Information Cards, series 1329, box 15, RG 75, National Archives, Washington, D.C.

4. "Nicholas Lassaw," Records of the Carlisle Indian Industrial School, Student Record Cards, series 1328, RG 75, National Archives, Washington, D.C.; Nicholas Lassaw Student Information Card, Records of the Carlisle Indian Industrial School, Student Record Cards, series 1329, box 15, RG 75, National Archives, Washington, D.C.

5. "Graduation Exercises Close Commencement Week," *The Carlisle Arrow* (Carlisle Indian School, Carlisle, Penna.), Apr. 10, 1914, p. 8.

6. "General School News," *The Carlisle Arrow*, Sept. 26, 1913, p. 3.

7. "Carlisle and Bucknell Battle to a Scoreless Tie," *The Carlisle Arrow*, Oct. 29, 1915, p. 2.

8. "General News Notes," *The Carlisle Arrow*, Nov. 5, 1915, p. 7.

9. "General News Notes," *The Carlisle Arrow*, Nov. 19, 1915, p. 6.

10. "General News Notes," *The Carlisle Arrow*, Sept. 29, 1916, p. 7.

11. "Indians Win Season's First Game," *The Carlisle Arrow and Red Man*, Oct. 5, 1917, p. 21.

12. "Nicholas Lassa, Left Tackle," *The Carlisle Arrow and Red Man*, Nov. 2, 1917, p. 15.

13. "General School News," *The Carlisle Arrow*, Jan. 8, 1915, p. 3; "Basketball," *The Carlisle Arrow and Red Man*, Feb. 22, 1918, p. 2.

14. "General School News," *The Carlisle Arrow*, Mar. 5, 1915, p. 2.

15. "General News Notes," *The Carlisle Arrow*, Feb. 18, 1916, p. 6.

16. "Orange Meet," *The Carlisle Arrow*, Apr. 6, 1917, p. 4; "Commencement Week Athletic Notes," *The Carlisle Arrow*, June 15, 1917, p. 2.

17. Clarence Welch, "Lebanon Valley Easily Defeated," *The Carlisle Arrow and Red Man*, Apr. 26, 1918, p. 1; "Carlisle 75, Gettysburg 51," *The Carlisle Arrow and Red Man*, May 10, 1918, p. 2; "The Athletic Reception," *The Carlisle Arrow and Red Man*, June 7, 1918, p. 22.

18. "General News Notes," *The Carlisle Arrow*, Jan. 28, 1916, p. 7.

19. "Athletic Notes," *The Carlisle Arrow*, Mar. 30, 1917, p. 2.

20. "General News Notes," *The Carlisle Arrow and Red Man*, Jan. 11, 1918, p. 3.

21. Maude Cooke, "The Holy Name Society," *The Carlisle Arrow*, March. 23, 1917, p. 3; C. M. Shunion. "Holy Name Society," *The Carlisle Arrow*, Jan. 18, 1918, p. 3; C. M. Shunion, "Holy Name Society," *The Carlisle Arrow and Red Man*, May 24, 1918, p. 2.

22. "General News Notes," *The Carlisle Arrow*, Mar. 10, 1916, p. 2.

23. "The Red Cross Branch at This School," *The Carlisle Arrow and Red Man*, Nov. 2, 1917, pp. 1-2; "Red Cross Notes," *The Carlisle Arrow and Red Man*, Dec. 21, 1917, p. 4; Father Phelan, "The Knights of Columbus War Camp Fund," *The Carlisle Arrow and Red Man*, Mar. 22, 1918, p. 2.

24. John Flinchum, "Invincibles," *The Carlisle Arrow*, Jan. 28, 1916, p. 6.

25. John Flinchum, "The Invincibles," *The Carlisle Arrow*, Feb. 4, 1916, p. 3.

26. Edwin K. Miller, "Standard Literary Society," *The Carlisle Arrow*, Feb. 11, 1916, p. 3; "The Invincibles," *The Carlisle Arrow*, Mar. 10, 1916, p. 6; Turner Dwight, "The Invincibles," *The Carlisle Arrow*, Mar. 17, 1916, p. 8.

27. Willie F. Goode, "The Invincibles," *The Carlisle Arrow*, Nov. 17, 1916, p. 7; "Joint Program Given by the Susans and Invincibles," *The Carlisle Arrow*, Dec. 22, 1916, p. 1; Herman Kelley, "The Invincibles," *The Carlisle Arrow*, Apr. 13, 1917, p. 8; "Invincibles Give Impressive Program," *The Carlisle Arrow*, May 4, 1917, p. 2.

28. James Holstein, "The Invincible Debating Society," *The Carlisle Arrow*, Sept. 14, 1917, p. 4; James Holstein, "The Invincible Debating Society," *The Carlisle Arrow*, Sept. 28, 1917, p. 3; "Red Cross Branch Organized at the School," *The Carlisle Arrow and Red Man*, Oct. 5, 1917, p. 18; George Pease, "Invincible Debating Society," *The Carlisle Arrow and Red Man*, Dec. 14, 1917, p. 3; Rupert Anderson, "Invincible Debating Society," *The Carlisle Arrow and Red Man*, Mar. 8, 1918, p. 3; Noah Hayes, "Invincible Debating Society," *The Carlisle Arrow and Red Man*, Apr. 19, 1918, p. 3.

29. "Armenian-Syrian Benefit Entertainment," *The Carlisle Arrow*, Nov. 24, 1916, p. 4; "American Indian Day," *The Carlisle Arrow*, May 11, 1917, p. 3; "General News Notes," *The Carlisle Arrow and Red Man*, Jan. 4, 1918, p. 23; "Patriotic Speeches," *The Carlisle Arrow and Red Man*, Apr. 19, 1918, p. 2.

30. "General News Notes," *The Carlisle Arrow*, Oct. 13, 1916, p. 3; "General News Notes," *The Carlisle Arrow*, Nov. 3, 1916, p. 4.

31. "Annual Athletic Banquet," *The Indian Leader* (Haskell Institute, Lawrence, Kansas), June 6-27, 1919, p. 63.

32. "As the Lawrence Reporters Saw the Game on September 27," *The Indian Leader*, Oct. 3, 1919, pp. 2-3.

33. "The Cincinnati Game," *The Indian Leader*, Dec. 5, 1919, p. 4.

34. "Notes of Notes," *The Indian Leader*, Feb. 20, 1920, p. 2.

35. "Notes of Interest," *The Indian Leader*, Oct. 1, 1920, p. 2.

36. "Haskell Defeated Hays Normal," *The Indian Leader*, Oct. 22, 1920, p. 5.

37. "Haskell Won a Hard Game from Marquette University," *The Indian Leader*, Nov. 12, 1920, p. 5.

38. "Religious Activities," *The Indian Leader*, Dec. 3, 1920, p. 3.

39. "Football Banquet," *The Indian Leader*, Dec. 10, 1920, pp. 2-3.

40. William Hampton, "Haskell's Successful Season," *The Indian Leader*, Dec. 31, 1920, pp. 14-15, 17.

41. "Athletic Banquet," *The Indian Leader*, June 3-17, 1921, p. 16.

42. "Haskell Triumphs Over Tulsa," *The Indian Leader*, Nov. 4, 1921, p. 4.

43. "Notes of the Game," *The Indian Leader*, Nov. 18, 1921, p. 4.

44. "Haskell Defeated College of Emporia," *The Indian Leader*, May 7, 1920, pp. 6-7.

45. "Inter-Society Track Meet," *The Indian Leader*, Apr. 1, 1921, p. 2.

46. "Haskell Athletes Won by a Large Score," *The Indian Leader*, Apr. 22, 1921, pp. 2-3.

47. "Haskell Won in a Dual Meet with the Aggies," *The Indian Leader*, May 13, 1921, p. 3.

48. "Religious Activities," *The Indian Leader*, Oct. 3, 1919, p. 3.

49. "Notes of Interest," *The Indian Leader*, May 28, 1920, p. 2.

50. "Religious Activities," *The Indian Leader*, Dec. 3, 1920, p. 3.

51. "Religious Activities," *The Indian Leader*, Jan. 28, 1921, p. 22.

52. "Officer's Party," *The Indian Leader*, Nov. 19, 1920, p. 1.

53. "Graduating Exercise," *The Indian Leader*, June 3-17, 1921, pp. 3-4; Nicholas Lassa, "The How and Why of Trade Training at Haskell," *The Indian Leader*, June 3-17, 1921, pp. 8-9.

54. "Ollanta," *The Indian Leader*, June 3-17, 1921, pp. 6-7.

55. "Class Day Program," *The Indian Leader*, June 3-17, 1921, p. 11; "Annual Alumni Dinner," *The Indian Leader*, June 3-17, 1921, p. 15.

56. See Robert L. Whitman, *Jim Thorpe and the Oorang Indians: The N.F.L.'s Most Colorful Franchise* (Marion, Ohio: Robert L. Whitman and Marion County Historical Society, 1984), pp. 42-87.

57. Whitman, *Jim Thorpe and the Oorang Indians*, pp. 83-87; Ron Cass, "Long Time Sleep," *Newsfile: Marion's Weekly Newsmagazine* (Marion, Ohio), Feb. 2, 1981, pp. 11, 13, 15, 19.

58. Confederated Salish and Kootenai Tribes Tribal Council minutes, Apr. 16, 1938, and Apr. 27, 1938, Confederated Salish and Kootenai Tribes, Pablo, Montana.

59. Maggie Plummer, "Long Time Sleep: The Stuff Legends Are Made Of," *Char-Koosta News* (Pablo, Mont.) Oct. 25, 2007, pp. 4-5; "Nickola Lassow Rites Monday," *The Missoulian*, Sept. 6, 1964, p. 13, c. 5.

Chapter 4
Jimmy Dupuis:
Flathead Reservation Fistic Warrior,
1930–1940

Between 1930 and 1940, Confederated Salish and Kootenai Tribes member Jimmy Dupuis was a staple in the boxing
scene of western Montana and the surrounding area. James Carl
Dupuis, the son of Orson Samuel Dupuis and Ann Pablo Dupuis, was born on December 16, 1909.[1]

Most of his 43 known bouts were fought in the Loyola
gym in Missoula. Of Dupuis' 43 bouts that were documented
in the local newspapers or listed in the official boxing records,
he won 22, lost 11, and fought 10 draws.[2] In the first half of the
1930s, Billy McFarland assembled and promoted cards of boxing matches at Loyola. McFarland was backed by two Missoula
businessmen, Orin Dishman and Max Yandt. In the early 1930s,
boxing was popular in Missoula and other Montana communities in the Bitterroot Valley, Flathead Valley, and Butte.[3]

According to an account related years later by Deane Jones,
one of Dupuis' early opponents,

> Jimmy Dupuis had powerful arms, power-
> ful shoulders, and guts no end. But he had one
> bad leg, a legacy of polio in childhood, and he
> couldn't step around with the footwork of a Fan-
> cy Dan. All he did was march forward and club
> the heck out of his opponents. I think I hit him
> with hundreds of left hands during the fight,
> stepping away as he swung. He'd just blink his
> eyes, stand there and wave at me to come and let

him catch me. In the final round I stood there
and traded punches with him."
Dupuis was so dedicated to his sport that he walked and hitch-
hiked the fifteen miles between Ronan and Polson to appear in a
bout at Polson one evening.[4]

Dupuis' first documented fight was at Loyola in Missoula
on December 12, 1930. The newspaper account emphasized Dupuis' resolve, determination, and endurance:

> While "Buck" Van Doren had a shade in
> the first two rounds, tough Jimmy Dupuis of
> Ronan socked him so hard and often in the last
> chapter that he won the decision. Van Dorn fired
> a hard right for a quick knockdown in the first
> seconds and led until the final stage. Then he
> wore out under Dupuis' frenzied outburst. The
> decision was unanimous.[5]

In the January 20, 1931, match between Dupuis and
Deane Jones, Jones "threw a hundred punches into chubby Jimmy Dupuis in the first two rounds." Deane won the match on a
two to one decision by the judges.[6]

Dupuis' stalwart spirit showed in his February 23, 1931,
Missoula fight with Clarence Cunningham: "At times it seemed
that neither would be able to withstand such punishment, but
both stayed on their feet under the heavy artillery, proving their
gameness as well as punching ability in a battle in which de-
fensive tactics were entirely forsaken." Dupuis and Cunningham
fought this match to a draw.[7]

In his next bout on April 21, 1931, Dupuis lost a decision
to Lee Morin. According to the *Daily Missoulian*, Morin won "in
six furious slugging rounds."[8]

On June 16, 1931, Dupuis knocked out Frank Van Dorn
in the second round of their re-match in Missoula.[9] That fall, on
October 21, 1931, Dupuis knocked out Dave Hildrich in Missoula and on October 30, 1931, Dupuis won a decision over Ray
Parker of Butte in a match fought in Butte.[10]

Dupuis had a ten-pound weight advantage over George Neva in their November 24, 1931, bout at Loyola in Missoula. The newspaper reported, "For vicious action no bout in recent months has matched that in which Chief Dupuis and George Neva battled to a draw."[11]

For the first time on January 20, 1932, Dupuis' fight against Nick Radick of Butte was the headline event on a Loyola fight card. Previously, his fights had been second or third on the card. During this fight, Dupuis administered "a systematic campaign waged incessantly through five vicious rounds" causing Nick Radick "to surrender halfway in the sixth."[12] Dupuis' stamina and endurance at his March 2, 1932, match against Eddie Coyle of Missoula impressed the audience: "The Flathead Indian assimilated everything that Coyle swung without breaking ground, and kept boring in."[13]

But Dupuis was knocked out by Dixie Lahood of Butte on April 15, 1932, in a fight in Butte.[14] Dupuis battled Eddie Coyle to a draw in their second meeting on December 16, 1932, at Loyola. Dupuis' was not the lead fight for the December 16, 1932, boxing card.[15]

On March 25, 1933, Dupuis battled Howard Hamel of Charlo in Charlo.[16] Dupuis fought George Neva to a draw on October 21, 1933, in Missoula.[17] Dupuis went on to lose a savage fight "unsurpassed for ferocity of the hard-punching contestants" to Cal (Branding Iron) Linn of Missoula on January 18, 1934.[18] On March 1, 1934, Dupuis lost a unanimous decision to Ray "Tiger" Cote of Butte when they fought in Missoula. The newspaper called it "an epochal struggle of two savage demons."[19] Dupuis won a decision against Sonny O'Day of Butte on April 12, 1934.[20]

In a re-match on March 17, 1934, Dupuis won "a spectacular third round victory" from Howard Hamel in a match fought in Polson.[21] Dupuis won a unanimous decision over Hamel in their third match on June 7, 1934, at Missoula. The newspaper reported Dupuis launched "a strenuous attack in the last two rounds" that "gave the crowd a taste for blood."[22]

During Missoula's 1934 Fourth of July celebration, Dupuis fought Bruce Kelley to a draw: "Both threw science away at moments for blood-lusty punching."[23] Dupuis had a fourth rematch with Howard Hamel of Charlo on Labor Day, September 3, 1934, in Ronan. Dupuis and Hamel "gave a splendid exhibition of aggressive battling in their six rounds." Dupuis "kept his foe on the move practically every minute of the encounter but could not land a haymaker." Dupuis won the decision with support from two of the three judges.[24]

A couple of weeks later on September 15, 1934, Dupuis lost a match with Tiger Cote of Butte fought in Hamilton.[25] In a four-round preliminary bout at Polson on September 28, 1934, Dupuis won a decision in a fight against Eddy Miller of Charlo.[26]

During 1935, Dupuis met "Spider" McCallum the boxing instructor at the Civilian Conservation Corps camp at Ninemile, Montana, at least four times, and fought one time against McCallum's brother Battling McCallum. Dupuis won his February 20, 1935, fight with Spider McCallum at Loyola in Missoula.[27] On June 20, 1935, Dupuis beat Battling McCallum in Missoula.[28] Dupuis got a draw with Spider McCallum on August 8, 1935, in Stevensville.[29] Dupuis lost a six-round decision against Spider McCallum in Hamilton on August 24, 1935.[30] In their final bout on August 30, 1935, Dupuis "was unable to continue after being struck a low blow by Spider McCallum . . . and [Dupuis] took the decision."[31]

In March 1935, Dupuis missed a fight because he was in the hospital. The newspaper report gave no details, but suggested the injury occurred in a fight.[32]

Dupuis fought Jimmy Reed of Portland to a draw at Loyola gym on September 25, 1935. According to the newspaper, they "knocked the daylights out of each other," and "When Jimmy [Dupuis] wasn't on the floor from terrific wallops, Reed reposed on the canvas after catching crashing blows."[33]

On December 13, 1935, Dupuis fought Charles Roper of Butte to a draw in the Loyola gum. The newspaper had Roper out boxing Dupuis at times, but Roper lost ground on low blows:

"Science was tossed into the discard by two lusty sockers who earned applause with their murderous intent."[34] Dupuis fought Charles Roper again in Spokane in March 1936 but lost that bout.[35]

Dupuis dropped out of the Missoula sports news in 1936. He parted ways with his Missoula promoters and signed up with promoters from Spokane: "Jimmy threw the Missoula promoters down," and "Jimmy Dupuis left a sad vacancy on the [Missoula] card by skipping to Spokane."[36] Dupuis did make the court news in 1936 for drunk and disorderly conduct. He was fined $10 for being drunk and disorderly in Lake County in November and again in December 1936.[37]

In 1937, Dupuis was back in the game and fought Butch Leiback from the small town of Dooley, Montana, in Hamilton, on June 5, 1937. Dupuis won the decision.[38] He also won a four-round decision from Buster Donaldson of Hamilton on June 24, 1937, in a fight at Hamilton.[39]

Dupuis saw action on April 4, 1938, in a celebration at Valley Creek near Arlee, Montana. He boxed Julian Pablo of Ronan to a draw.[40] The last Dupuis bout to make the Missoula news was a March 28, 1940, fight with Johnny Adams in Kellogg, Idaho. The fight was fought in Kellogg and Dupuis lost the decision.[41]

According to one source, Dupuis turned to wrestling after he quit boxing. Between December 11, 1941, and September 17, 1943, he served in the U.S. Army. He lived in the Seattle area in his later years and died in Washington on December 12, 1972.[42]

Endnotes

1. Eugene Felsman to Bob Bigart, Feb. 15, 2022, email.

2. "Jimmy Dupuis," BoxRec.com, accessed Feb. 17, 2022.

3. John T. Campbell, "Montana's Boxers Recalled," *The Missoulian*, Dec. 14, 1982, p. 12; John T. Campbell, "A Salute of 'Mr. Boxing,'" *Missoulian*, Apr. 14, 1985, p. 21.

4. Deane Jones, "Keeping Up with Jones," *The Missoulian*, Dec. 30, 1971, p. 7.

5. "Neva Stops Eide in Fourth Round . . . .," *The Daily Missoulian*, Dec. 13, 1930, p. 8, c. 3.

6. "Neva Wins Decision in Slashing Fray with Hissong," *The Daily Missoulian*, Jan. 21, 1931, p. 6, c. 1.

7. "Neva's Attack in Last Two Rounds Gains Decision," *The Daily Missoulian*, Feb. 24, 1931, p. 6, c. 1.

8. "Neva Wins Decision in Spirited Battle with Cole," *The Daily Missoulian*, Apr. 22, 1931, p. 6, c. 1-2.

9. "Lenhart Wins Unanimous Decision from Soldier Foe," *The Daily Missoulian*, June 17, 1931, p. 6, c. 1.

10. "Cunningham and Neva Fight Wicked Draw in Windup," *The Daily Missoulian*, Oct. 22, 1931, p. 6, c. 1; "Dupuis Defeats Butte Battler," *The Daily Missoulian*, Oct. 31, 1931, p. 8, c. 5.

11. "Smith Wins Decision; Neva and Indian in Fierce Draw," *The Daily Missoulian*, Nov. 25, 1931, p. 6, c. 1.

12. "Jimmy Dupuis; McKay, Win with Constant Attack," *The Daily Missoulian*, Jan. 21, 1932, p. 3, c. 1.

13. "Dupuis, M'Kay, Neva Win Hard Contests," *The Daily Missoulian*, Mar. 3, 1932, p. 3, c. 5-6.

14. "Lahood Is Winner Over Dupuis," *The Daily Missoulian*, Apr. 16, 1932, p. 7, c. 1.

15. "Smith, Kelley Win Decisions; Linn Lands a Knockout," *The Daily Missoulian*, Dec. 17, 1932, p. 6, c. 1.

16. Ray T. Rocene, "Sport Jabs," *The Daily Missoulian*, Mar. 25, 1933, p. 3, c. 2-3.

17. "Del Fontaine Wins by Quick Knockout," *The Daily Missoulian*, Oct. 21, 1933, p. 7, c. 1.

18. "Two Fierce Bouts Two Knockouts At Strong Ring Card," *The Daily Missoulian*, Jan. 19, 1934, p. 6, c. 7-8.

19. "Fontaine Takes Title; Cote Wins Savage Encounter," *The Daily Missoulian*, Mar. 2, 1934, p. 6, c. 1.

20. "Fontaine Easy Winner; Linn, Dupuis Score Decisions," *The Daily Missoulian*, Apr. 13, 1934, p. 8, c. 1.

21. "Polson Fans Enjoy Fast Boxing Card," *The Daily Missoulian*, Mar. 20, 1934, p. 3, c. 3.

22. "Dupuis Wins Only Decision, With Four Bouts Draws," *The Daily Missoulian,* June 8, 1934, p. 6, c. 1.

23. "Celebration Hits Peak Today," *The Daily Missoulian*, July 4, 1934, p. 1, c. 7-8, and p. 2, c. 1-2.

24. "Annual Celebration Attracts Big Crowd," *The Ronan Pioneer*, Sept. 6, 1934, p. 1, c. 1-2.

25. "Cote Gets Nod in Bout at Hamilton," *The Daily Missoulian*, Sept. 16, 1934, p. 6, c. 8.

26. "Hoxwood Knocks Out Cut Bank Opponent," *The Daily Missoulian*, Sept. 29, 1934, p. 2, c. 7-8.

27. "Lightweights Rip Through a Savage Conflict to Draw," *The Daily Missoulian*, Feb. 21, 1935, p. 6, c. 3-4.

28. "Fontaine Wins Decisively in Return Title Match," *The Daily Missoulian,* June 21, 1935, p. 9, c. 1.

29. "Fontaine Winner from Game Boy in Valley Clash," *The Daily Missoulian,* Aug. 9, 1935, p. 8, c. 5-6.

30. "McCallum Victor Over Dupuis in Hamilton Match," *The Daily Missoulian,* Aug. 25, 1935, p. 8, c. 2.

31. "Fontaine Whips Palmore in Savage 10-Round Thriller," *The Daily Missoulian,* Aug. 31, 1935, p. 6, c. 1.

32. "Strong, Fast Featherweights Fight in Windup Tonight," *The Daily Missoulian,* Mar. 20, 1935, p. 3, c. 1.

33. "Slambang Scrap of Dupuis, Reed Is Brightest Spot," *The Daily Missoulian,* Sept. 26, 1935, p. 6, c. 7.

34. "Fontaine and Dennis Battle Fiercely to a Draw Decision in Windup," *The Daily Missoulian*, Dec. 14, 1935, p. 9, c. 6.

35. Ray T. Rocene, "Sport Jabs," *The Daily Missoulian*, Mar. 24, 1936, p. 6, c. 2-4.

36. Ray T. Rocene, "Sport Jabs," *The Daily Missoulian*, Mar. 19, 1936, p. 8, c. 2-4; Ray T. Rocene, "Sport Jabs," *The Daily Missoulian*, Mar. 22, 1936, p. 8, c. 2-6.

37. "County, City Police Busy, and the Game Warden; Past Week," *The Flathead Courier* (Polson, Mont.), Nov. 12, 1936, p. 5, c. 3; "Jail Sentences and Fines for Violators," *The Flathead Courier*, Dec. 17, 1936, p. 1, c. 5.

38. "Smith, Lindgren Battle to Draw," *The Daily Missoulian*, June 6, 1937, p. 7, c. 4.

39. "Smith Beats Jenkins," *The Daily Missoulian*, June 25, 1937, p. 2, c. 5.

40. "Record Crowd at Valley Creek for ECW Birthday," *The Daily Missoulian,* Apr. 7, 1938, p. 7, c. 1.

41. "McCallum Upsets Portland Boxer with Hard Right," *The Daily Missoulian*, Mar. 29, 1940, p. 2, c. 4-5.

42. Deane Jones, "Keeping Up with Jones," *The Missoulian*, Dec. 30, 1971, p. 7; Eugene Felsman to Bob Bigart, Feb. 15, 2022, email.

Chapter 5
Frenchy Roullier and Sam Clairmont: Ronan Athletic Stars, 1925–1940

Two Confederated Salish and Kootenai Tribal members, Phillip "Frenchy" Roullier and Alexander "Sam" Clairmont, dominated Ronan High School basketball history between 1925 and 1929. In 1929, the Ronan team placed third in the Montana State basketball tournament which then included all high schools in the state, regardless of size. Roullier played forward and Clairmont was center for the team. In the 1920s there was a jump ball after every basket was made, which made the center an especially important team member.[1] Another tribal member, Theodore "Bias" Stinger, was also on the team.

Alexander Clairmont was born in Pablo on September 12, 1908, to Alphonse and Armine Morigeau Clairmont. Phillip Roullier was born in Ronan on September 19, 1910, to Fred and Caroline Ethier Roullier.[2]

Ronan High School, 1925–1929

In 1926 the Ronan team played in the district basketball tournament in Missoula, but lost to Loyola High School, Missoula, and St. Regis High School.[3] The 1926–1927 Ronan team lost to Loyola and beat Frenchtown and Polson during the regular season. In the Frenchtown game on January 23, 1927, Roullier and Kenneth Egan, a non-Indian teammate, were the "star players." In defeating Thompson Falls 30 to 22 on February 4, 1927, Roullier and Egan each scored 13 points and Clairmont got 6. In the Polson game on February 7, 1927, Ronan won 27 to 24. Roullier was the high scorer with 17 points and Clairmont was second with 9 points.[4]

Ronan lost to Loyola 16 to 18 in a low scoring game played in Ronan on February 19, 1927. Roullier was again high scorer with 9 points; Clairmont got 4.[5] Ronan beat Alberton on February 18, 1927, 28 to 22. Roullier and Clairmont each got 8 points against Alberton, but Egan scored 10 points.[6]

At the district tournament in Missoula in 1927, Ronan lost to Loyola, 19 to 22 in the championship game. Roullier got 11 points, Egan 6, and Clairmont 2.[7]

The 1927–1928 Ronan High School basketball team was again dominated by Roullier, Clairmont, and Egan. This team made it to the Montana State Tournament and had a 20 to 8 winning record.[8] On December 23, 1927, Ronan beat Dixon 42 to 15 and Clairmont was high scorer for Ronan with 21 points.[9] Ronan beat Thompson Falls 28 to 23 on January 5, 1928, and Roullier was the high scorer with 12 points.[10]

The big news was on February 3, 1928, when Ronan beat traditional powerhouse Loyola, 22 to 15.[11] The 1927–1928 Ronan team was attracting attention and a *Daily Missoulian* columnist wrote:

> Roullier, the dead-shot basket tosser of the western district tournament last season, and young Egan, a brother of the original Ronan star, are making a flock of baskets in every game, with Clairmont, the tall Indian center, another bright light.[12]

Ronan High School won the 1928 Western Montana District championship played in Missoula. They beat St. Regis 47 to 30. According to the *Daily Missoulian*, "Roullier of Ronan with 30 points gave the outstanding display of individual playing so far in the first game on the University court [and the] . . . third quarter was one wild flurry of baskets by Roullier."[13] After defeating St. Ignatius 42 to 22, the Ronan team met Superior in the championship game which Ronan won 34 to 19. Roullier was the leading scorer for the tournament with 111 points.

Phillip "Frenchy" Roullier,
Ronan High School basketball, 1929.
Courtesy Rene Roullier-Madrigal, Ronan, Montana.

Alexander "Sam" Clairmont,
Ronan High School basketball, 1929.
Courtesy Rene Roullier-Madrigal, Ronan, Montana.

Clairmont ranked sixth with 55 points. The referees selected a western district tournament all-star team which included Roullier, Egan, and Clairmont.[14]

The Ronan High School team, then called the "Reservation Tornados," played in the Montana State Basketball Tournament in March 1928 in Butte. According to the *Ronan Pioneer*, Roullier was "the most versatile man in the squad, a marvelous ball rustler, floorman and basket-shooter."[15]

But there were some bumps in the road at the state tournament. Ronan lost to Great Falls 33 to 40 in their first game. The *Daily Missoulian* reported "Roullier tossed nine dazzling baskets, many of them long heaves, but alone could not match the sharp shooting Great Falls quint . . . [he had been] ill during the day, having a fever, but jumped out of bed to play great ball."[16] Ronan did go on to defeat Dillon 19 to 17 with Roullier leading "a flashy offense." Ronan went down to defeat in the championship game against Manhattan. Ronan lost that game 11 to 39: "Roullier was covered by two men all of the time."[17] Roullier scored a total of 30 points in the tournament.[18]

The 1928–1929 Ronan High School basketball team again featured Roullier, Egan, and Clairmont. That was the first Ronan team to be called the "Chiefs." Ray Rocene, a sports columnist for the *Daily Missoulian*, suggested the name because most of the team members were tribal members. The team had a 23 to 1 conference record in the 1928–1929 season.[19] Clairmont worked his way through school during the 1928–1929 school year by driving a school bus.[20]

During the regular season Ronan defeated Kalispell 53 to 16 on December 22, 1928. They outpointed Missoula County High School 37 to 16 on January 4, 1929. They won over Whitefish on January 11, 1929, 25 to 21. On January 14, 1929, they beat Polson 56 to 33. Ronan bested Thompson Falls on January 24, 1929, 39 to 17. Finally, on January 26, 1929, Ronan beat a different Whitefish team, 46 to 24.[21]

On February 2, 1929, however, the university's super-varsity team beat Ronan 32 to 25: "Roullier, Ronan forward, and

Clairmont, center, were the best threats of the Ronan crew. Roullier looking like real high school class."[22] Then Ronan defeated Thompson Falls 50 to 6 on February 8, 1929, and Plains 59 to 18 on February 15, 1929.[23] As of February 10, 1929, Roullier had scored 264 points during the season, Egan 218, and Clairmont, 138.[24]

According to Ray Rocene, *Daily Missoulian* sports columnist, "'Frenchy' Roullier, the agile Ronan forward, has scored 275 points for his team this season [as of February 21, 1929]. Watch him go. While the University boys who have played against Sam Clairmont, the tall Indian center of the Chiefs, speak very well of him, as a jumper and floorman."[25]

In February 1929 the Ronan team brushed through the district tournament in Missoula. They beat Thompson Falls 50 to 5; Frenchtown 36 to 19; Plains 44 to 9; and Plains a second time 40 to 14.[26] In the championship game, "Clairmont had the misfortune to badly sprain an ankle. After the injury was taped Clairmont went in and finished the game, and was high point man in spite of the injury. Until a day or two ago he has been forced to use crutches and the local fans are earnestly hoping that he will entirely recover before the state tournament."[27] Before the state tournament Roullier had scored 376 points, Egan 290, and Clairmont 212.[28]

Clairmont was back with the team on March 6, 1929, when Ronan beat Great Falls 32 to 30 in Bozeman. Ronan had led by 10 points, but Great Falls rallied late in the game. The *Daily Missoulian* reported, "Control of the tipoff by Clairmont was a feature of Ronan's play, while Roullier was easily the best forward."[29] Ronan then beat Manhattan 39 to 14: "Roullier contributed the finest individual play of the tournament in the fastest exhibition yet offered the fans, with Clairmont and Egan supporting him in spectacular style."[30]

Unfortunately for the Ronan team, they were defeated by Butte Central 22 to 35 in the semifinals. Then Ronan beat Anaconda 31 to 25 to take third place in the tournament.[31] Despite the loss, Roullier was a unanimous choice by the tournament committee as part of the all-tournament team.[32] The Ronan team was recognized as the "cleanest playing" of the tournament. They had the fewest fouls of any team, and no players fouled out.[33]

Roullier and Clairmont also starred in track events during their 1925 to 1929 high school career. At the Lake County track meet on May 21, 1926, Clairmont placed second in the shot put and Roullier was third in the javelin throw.[34] At the Lake County track meet on May 5, 1928, Ronan won first place. Roullier tied for third in the pole vault and placed second in the half-mile race. Clairmont got second in the shot put.[35] Ronan also took first place in the May 20, 1929, Lake County track meet. Clairmont got first in the low hurdles and second in the shot put. Roullier tied for first in the pole vault, took first in the javelin throw, and won the one-mile race.[36]

The Ronan basketball stars also joined some other activities. On May 9, 1927, Roullier was an actor in a student play called "The Touchdown."[37] Roullier also served as a male model for the Ronan Woman's Club fashion show on April 19, 1928.[38] Roullier and Clairmont graduated from Ronan High School in May 1929.[39] As president of the senior class, Clairmont presided over the class day exercises on May 22, 1929. Roullier was part of a quartet that sang a song, "Farewell," at the exercises.[40]

Mount St. Charles College, 1929–1931.

In 1929, Frenchy Roullier, Sam Clairmont, and Kenneth Egan enrolled in Mount St. Charles College in Helena. The college later changed its name to Carroll College. The Ronan triumvirate dominated the Mount St. Charles sports scene for 1929–1930, but only Roullier was able to attend a second year, 1930–1931.

Clairmont and Roullier went out for football in Helena. Roullier played his first game on October 19, 1929, in a 0 to 6 loss to the Billings Polytechnic Institute. The student newspaper wrote that Roullier "showed plenty of class, and will provide fine material for varsity teams in future years."[41] Roullier also played for the Mount St. Charles Fighting Saints during the 1930 football season. Among other plays, Roullier "made an amazing catch" in an October 17, 1930, 9 to 0 win over an independent football team from Butte. On November 8, 1930, in a 13 to 13 tie game with Brigham Young University at Butte, Roullier showed "plenty of promise for coming seasons." Roullier played in the left halfback position.[42]

But the Ronan recruits had their biggest impact on Mountain St. Charles' basketball team in 1929 and 1930. In a December 1929 loss to the Montana State College Bobcats, "Roullier, former Ronan flash, was high point man for the Saints. He did sensational work in the first game carrying, with [William] Gross, the full offensive work. He scored 10 of the points accumulated by the Saint aggregation."[43]

In January 1930, Mount St. Charles played two losing games against the Montana University Grizzlies 34 to 41 and 32 to 63. In the first game Clairmont and Egan scored "sensational shots from mid-floor." In the second game, however, "Roullier, whose shoulder had been injured in the game the night before showed a marked letup in his style of play and accounted for only two of the Saints total."[44]

Mount St. Charles lost two games to Gonzaga on January 17 and 18, 1930. In the first game Clairmont and Roullier "showed up well with some wonderful team play and a good offensive." In the second game Roullier with William Gross scored the great majority of the Saints' baskets.[45]

In February 1930, Mount St. Charles won one of two additional games they played against Gonzaga. Gonzaga won the first of this series, but "Roullier broke lose to sink one of his famous short shots to cut the lead to one point." Roullier scored 14 points, but Gonzaga won this game 47 to 46. In the last game, "The Gonzagans kept Roullier under a double guard all of the evening but they failed to account for [Kenneth] Egan." Egan went on the make 19 points as Mount St. Charles beat Gonzaga 42 to 39.[46] Also in February 1930, Mount St. Charles won two games against Whitman College with "Roullier, Gross, Egan and

Clairmont hitting the basket with sickening regularity for the Saints . . . . Gross and Roullier, with Clairmont and Egan played wonderful offensive ball."[47]

Roullier played basketball for the 1930–1931 Mount St. Charles College Saints, but Clairmont did not attend a second year. The Saints opened the season with a two-game loss to the Montana State College Bobcats starting on December 8, 1930. In the first game, "Roullier was the outstanding player on the floor. He scored 14 of the 18 points the Saints made." Roullier's "speed and general ability secured the lead for the Saints in the initial period" of the second game, but the Saints lost the second game 33 to 40.[48] On December 19 and 20, 1930, the St. Charles team played two more games against the Bobcats and lost them both, 26 to 48 and 22 to 42.[49]

St. Charles beat the Helena Eagles on January 27, 1931, 27 to 26. At the end of the game "Roullier sank a perfect basket that spelled victory and ended the scoring." Roullier scored 19 points in that game.[50] A few days later on January 31, 1931, the Saints played against the Montana School of Mines Hilltoppers. Roullier scored 18 points in the Saints' 45 to 24 win in the first game. On February 10, 1931, Roullier scored ten points in a second game with the Hilltoppers. But the Saints lost the second game 17 to 19.[51]

On February 21, 1931, St. Charles closed out the basketball season with a 38 to 20 victory over Intermountain: "Roullier seemed to have an off night until toward the end when he broke fast and often to score four goals and sew up the game for the Saints."[52]

In addition to starring in basketball, Frenchy Roullier and Sam Clairmont played on the Mount St. Charles horseshoe teams. According to the student newspaper, "Clairmont seems to be the most consistent performer of the tourney with his running mate Kierman close behind. Both had been tossing ringers consistently and are going to be hard to beat."[53] In 1965, Sam Clairmont was inducted into Carroll College's basketball hall of fame.[54]

Independent Basketball Teams, 1931–1940

By the fall of 1931 both Roullier and Clairmont had dropped out of Mount St. Charles College, but they did not retire from basketball. In the 1930s many Montana communities had business sponsored or independent basketball teams that were separate from the high school or college teams. During the 1931–1932 season, Frenchy Roullier played for a Polson team sponsored by Boettcher Hardware in Polson. On November 28, 1931, Roullier scored 15 points as the Boettcher team defeated the Missoula Hamburger Kings 26 to 16.[55]

In December 1931, Roullier was playing with another independent team from Helena called the Eagles. Roullier scored six points, but the Eagles lost in Helena to a Montana State alumni team 21 to 62.[56] In March 1932 the Polson team was called the Polson Independents and included Clairmont as a player. The Independents took fourth place in a tournament of independent basketball teams held in Helena.[57] On March 13, 1932, Mr. and Mrs. W. C. Boettcher entertained the Polson Independents, including Clairmont, at dinner.[58]

In the 1932–1933 season, the Polson Independents beat a Somers team 43 to 11. Roullier was second highest scorer for the Independents with 14 points and Clairmont was third with 9 points.[59] Later in December 1932, they beat Whitefish 35 to 28. Roullier was the lead scorer with 14 points.[60] The Independents, featuring Roullier, played the Montana State University Grizzly basketball team in Missoula on January 7, 1933. The Independents lost that game 44 to 52.[61]

As of February 9, 1933, the Polson team had played 21 games that season and won 19. Roullier was the high scorer with 261 points and Clairmont was third with 163 before February 1933.[62] Roullier scored 30 points on February 21, 1933, as the Polson team romped over Alberton, 67 to 25.[63]

The Polson Independents went on to defeat the Daily Company team of Missoula (31-28) and a team called the Cubs (39-31) later in February 1933. Roullier was the lead Polson scorer in both games.[64] Clairmont also played for the Polson

Independents for the 1934–1935 season. At a February 1935 tournament of independent teams, Clairmont was the lead scorer with 34 points.[65]

In the 1935–1936 season the Polson Independents beat the Standard Oilers of Kalispell twice, 48 to 33 and 49 to 38, in December 1935. In the second game, Clairmont was the high scorer with 20 points and Roullier was second with 13 points.[66] In January 1936, Polson beat Alberton, 27 to 20. Roullier was high scorer with 10 points and Clairmont had 6 points.[67]

In 1935 the Polson Independents won first place in the Western Montana Independent Basketball Tournament and in 1936 they placed second.[68] On December 11, 1936, Polson played the Montana State University Grizzlies in Missoula. A *Daily Missoulian* columnist commented that Clairmont and Roullier "know how to shoot. The last time they played here [Missoula] they might have won had Roullier not been lost on fouls early in the second half."[69] The Grizzlies won 61 to 23 despite Polson being ahead at one point in the game. Roullier scored 4 points and Clairmont 7.[70]

In 1940, Clairmont and Roullier were with the Flathead Agency Independent basketball team. As of January 21, 1940, the Flathead Agency team had played nine games and were undefeated. Frenchy Roullier and Sam Clairmont were the stars of the team.[71] The Agency team played in the Western Montana Independent Tournament in Missoula in late January 1940. They defeated a team from Corvallis 43 to 37, but they were eliminated from the tournament after a 26 to 28 loss to a team from the Haugen Civilian Conservation Corps camp.[72]

Frenchy Roullier and Sam Clairmont cooperated in other activities as well as basketball. In December 1935 both ran for election to the first tribal council under the new Indian Reorganization Act government. Clairmont was elected to the council from Dixon, but Roullier was not successful in his contest to represent Ronan.[73] They fished and hunted together in 1937.[74]

Both Roullier and Clairmont worked for the Bureau of Indian Affairs and Confederated Salish and Kootenai Tribes at

Top: Phillip "Frenchy" Roullier, U.S. Army, 1944-1946.
Bottom: Phillip "Frenchy" Roullier and
Lucille Trosper Roullier, 1939.
Courtesy Rene Roullier-Madrigal, Ronan, Montana.

Dixon Agency and were active in organizing social events among the employees.[75] In 1937 Sam Clairmont got the lowest score in a golf match at the Flathead club course at Dixon. They were both members of the Reservation Golf Club in 1942.[76] Their cooperative endeavors ended with Frenchy Roullier's death in June 1955. Sam Clairmont was one of his pallbearers.[77]

Life Beyond Basketball: Phillip "Frenchy" Roullier

In the late 1930s, Roullier worked at the Flathead Agency as property clerk.[78] In 1944 and 1945, he served in the U.S. Army and was discharged in 1946 as staff sergeant.[79]

After serving in the army, Roullier was appointed manager of the tribal mineral bathhouse at Hot Springs. In 1948 and 1949 the tribe built a new bathhouse facility as an economic enterprise. The dedication of the new building in July 1949 brought in the governor of Montana and featured Jim Thorpe, the famous Indian athlete.[80]

Roullier was active in community affairs in Hot Springs and served as co-chairman of the annual Homesteader Day celebration and president of the Hot Springs Chamber of Commerce. He was appointed as a member of the Montana State Chamber of Commerce travel board in 1950.[81]

On June 13, 1955, Roullier was admitted to the Hot Springs hospital with a heart condition and he died later the same morning. He was only 44 years old. He was survived by his second wife, Lucille Trosper Roullier, and two daughters. The funeral at Ronan attracted a large crowd from across the reservation.[82]

Life After Basketball: Alexander "Sam" Clairmont

Alexander "Sam" Clairmont survived his sports partner by 37 years and died in 1992. After leaving Mount St. Charles College in 1930, Clairmont studied forestry at Fort Simco in White Swan, Washington. In 1931, he was employed by the Bureau of Indian Affairs Forestry Department on the Flathead

Top: Alexander "Sam" Clairmont in hunting camp, 1954.
Courtesy Rene Roullier-Madrigal, Ronan, Montana.
Bottom: Alexander "Sam" Clairmont,
Courtesy Confederated Salish and Kootenai Tribes, Tribal
Council, Pablo, Montana.

Reservation. He retired from the Bureau of Indian Affairs land services in 1968.[83]

In 1935 Clairmont was elected as the Dixon representative on the new Confederated Salish and Kootenai Tribes council. He served on the council until 1939.[84] Between 1939 and 1942, Clairmont was on the board of directors of the Lake County Sportsmen's Association.[85]

Clairmont was elected to the Dixon school board in 1952.[86] That same year, Clairmont was a witness in the Confederated Salish and Kootenai Tribes' case in the Indian Claims Commission.[87] In 1958 Clairmont was elected president of the Dixon Schools' Parent-Teacher Association.[88]

After retiring from the Bureau of Indian Affairs in 1968, he worked for the Confederated Salish and Kootenai Tribes setting up the tribal realty department. Clairmont died at his home near Polson on March 24, 1992, at the age of 83. He was survived by his wife, two sons, and three daughters.[89]

From the late 1920s to the 1990s, Phillip "Frenchy" Roullier and Alexander "Sam" Clairmont combined athletic talent with public service. They played important roles in the establishment and growth of the early Confederated Salish and Kootenai Tribes tribal government and the tribal community during much of the twentieth century.

Endnotes

1. Jim Clairmont to Rene Roullier-Madrigal, May 2022, personal communication.

2. "Phillip Alfred 'Frenchy' Roullier" and "Alexander 'Sam' Leonard Clairmont," Eugene Felsman, Confederated Salish and Kootenai Tribes family group sheets, McNickle Library, Salish Kootenai College, Pablo, Montana.

3. Gale Decker, *Over-Time: A History of Ronan High School Boys' & Girls' Basketball* (privately printed, n. d.), p. 40.

4. "Loyola Five Stops Ronan, Score 23 to 13," *The Ronan Pioneer*, Jan. 13, 1927, p. 1, c. 5; "Ronan Defeats Fast Frenchtown Team in a Second Game," *The Ronan Pioneer*, Jan. 27, 1927, p. 1, c. 6; "Ronan Five Beats Polson, By 27 to 24," *The Ronan Pioneer*, Feb. 8, 1927, p. 6, c. 3; "Ronan Hoop Teams Take Three Straight," *The Ronan Pioneer*, Feb. 10, 1927, p. 8, c. 4.

5. "Loyola Takes Close Contest from Ronan," *The Daily Missoulian*, Feb. 20, 1927, p. 4, c. 5.

6. "Alberton Loses First Game to Ronan Five," *The Ronan Pioneer*, Feb. 24, 1927, p 1, c. 3.

7. "Ronan Loses to Loyola in Fiercely Fought Contest," *The Ronan Pioneer*, Mar. 3, 1927, p. 1, c. 1-3.

8. Decker, *Over-Time*, p. 41.

9. "Ronan Hoopsters Take Two Games," *The Daily Missoulian*, Dec. 25, 1927, p. 6, c. 6.

10. "Ronan Wins in Game with Thompson Falls," *The Daily Missoulian*, Jan. 9, 1928, p. 5, c. 6.

11. "Ronan Quint Defeats Loyola by 22–15 Score," *The Ronan Pioneer*, Feb. 9, 1928, p. 1, c. 5.

12. Ray Rocene, "Sport Jabs," *The Daily Missoulian*, Jan. 24, 1928, p. 7, c. 1-2.

13. "Ronan, Superior, Leading District Contenders," *The Daily Missoulian*, Feb. 24, 1928, p. 1, c. 6, and p. 9, c. 1-3.

14. "Ronan Lads Earn Western District Title. . . .," *The Daily Missoulian*, Feb. 26, 1928, p. 1, c. 1, and p. 9, c. 1-5.

15. "Ronan Basketball Quint Enters State Tournament," *The Ronan Pioneer*, Mar. 8, 1928, p. 1, c. 1.

16. "Ronan Is Nosed Out by Great Falls in Thrilling Contest, 40–33," *The Daily Missoulian*, Mar 9, 1928, p. 1, c. 7, and p. 8, c. 1-2.

17. "Missoula High Loses Hard Game to Billings," *The Daily Missoulian*, Mar. 10, 1928, p. 1, c. 6-7, and p. 6, c. 1-2.

18. "No Upsets Provided by Missoula, Ronan," *The Daily Missoulian*, Mar. 12, 1928, p. 3, c. 2-4.

19. Decker, *Over-Time*, pp. 41-42; Jim Clairmont to Rene Roullier-Madrigal, May 2022, personal communication.

20. "In the Past," *The Daily Missoulian*, Mar. 9, 1949, p. 4, c. 3.

21. "Ronan Chiefs Defeat Kalispell," *The Ronan Pioneer*, Dec. 27, 1928, p. 1, c. 1; "Ronan Chiefs Win in Game with Missoula," *The Ronan Pioneer*, Jan. 10, 1929, p. 1, c. 6; "Ronan Is Winner in Polson Clash," *The Daily Missoulian*, Jan. 15, 1929, p. 6, c. 2; "Ronan Chiefs Win All Games Yet Played," *The Ronan Pioneer*, Jan. 17, 1929, p. 1, c. 3; "Ronan Chiefs Win Two More Games," *The Ronan Pioneer*, Jan. 31, 1929, p. 1, c. 2.

22. "Ronan Loses Game to Super-Varsity," *The Daily Missoulian*, Feb. 3, 1929, p. 9, c. 3.

23. "Ronan Chiefs Win More Games," *The Ronan Pioneer*, Feb. 14, 1929, p. 1, c. 3; "Ronan Chiefs Defeat Plains," *The Ronan Pioneer*, Feb. 21, 1929, p. 1, c. 2.

24. "Western District Tourney Here February 21, 22, 23," *The Daily Missoulian*, Feb. 10, 1929, p. 9, c. 1.

25. Ray Rocene, "Sport Jabs," *The Daily Missoulian*, Feb. 21, 1929, p. 6, c. 2-4.

26. Decker, *Over-Time*, p. 41.

27. "Ronan Chiefs Easily Win Tournament," *The Ronan Pioneer*, Feb. 28, 1929, p. 1, c. 1.

28. "State Basketball Tourney Will Start Wednesday," *The Daily Missoulian*, Mar. 3, 1929, p. 9, c. 1-4.

29. "Ronan Defeats Great Falls in Thrilling Affray," *The Daily Missoulian*, Mar. 7, 1929, p. 6, c. 1.

30. "Ronan, Butte Central Meet in Semi-Finals Today," *The Daily Missoulian*, Mar. 9, 1929, p. 8, c. 1.

31. "Miles City Wins State Title," *The Daily Missoulian*, Mar. 10, 1929, p. 5, c. 1-4.

32. "Roullier of Ronan Unanimous Choice for Place on All-State Hoop Squad," *The Daily Missoulian*, Mar. 10, 1929, p. 6, c. 2-4.

33. "Record for Clean Playing Was Set by Ronan Boys," *The Daily Missoulian*, Mar. 13, 1929, p. 7, c. 1.

34. "Ronan Holds Lead in Lake County School Track Meet," *The Ronan Pioneer*, May 28, 1926, p. 1, c. 1-2.

35. "Ronan Takes County Field Meet," *The Daily Missoulian*, May 6, 1928, p. 6, c. 3-4.

36. "Ronan High School Wins First Prizes at Track Meet," *The Ronan Pioneer*, May 23, 1929, p. 1, c. 1-2, and p. 8, c. 2-3.

37. "The Touchdown," *The Ronan Pioneer*, Apr. 28, 1927, p. 1, c. 2-3.

38. "Fashion Show Feature of Season's Functions," *The Ronan Pioneer*, Apr. 26, 1928, p. 1, c. 2.

39. "Very Successful School Year Closes with 32 Graduates," *The Ronan Pioneer*, May 23, 1929, p. 1, c. 3.

40. "Ronan Society," *The Daily Missoulian*, May 26, 1929, ed. sec. p. 4, c. 3-4.

41. "St. Charles Reserves Lose 6-0 Scrimmage with Billings Poly," *The Prospector* (Mount St. Charles College, Helena, Mont.), Oct. 25, 1929, p. 3.

42. "Saint Gridders Defeat Englewood in Home Game," *The Prospector*, Nov. 22, 1930, p. 3; "B.Y.U. Ties St. Charles at Butte," *The Prospector*, Nov. 22, 1930, pp. 1 and 6.

43. "Saint Basketers to Cover Northwest While on Long Jaunt," *The Prospector*, Dec. 19, 1929, p. 3.

44. "Saints Lose Two Games to Strong Grizzlies," *The Prospector*, Jan. 30, 1930, p. 3.

45. "Gonzaga Beats Saints in Two Listless Games," *The Prospector*, Jan. 30, 1930, p. 3.

46. "Saints Split Two Games Series with Gonzagans," *The Prospector*, Feb. 22, 1930, pp. 3 and 6.

47. "Whitman Drops Two Hard Games to Saints," *The Prospector*, Feb. 22, 1930, p. 3.

48. "Basketball Season Opens with Bobcats Winning Two Games," *The Prospector*, Dec. 18, 1930, p. 3.

49. "Hilltoppers [sic] Drop Two Games to Montana State," *The Prospector*, Feb. 19, 1931, p. 3.

50. "Saints Nose Out Eagles in 27-26 Thrill Contest," *The Prospector*, Feb. 19, 1931, p. 3.

51. "Saints Exchange Games with School of Mines," *The Prospector*, Feb. 19, 1931, p. 3.

52. "Varsity Quint Ends Season with 38-40 Victory Over I.U.C.," *The Prospector*, Mar. 16, 1931, p. 3.

53. "Upsets Feature First Round of the Annual Horse Shoe Tourney," *The Prospector*, May 9, 1930, p. 4.

54. Jim Clairmont to Rene Roullier-Madrigal, May 2022, personal communication.

55. "Boettcher Quint Beats Hamburgers," *The Daily Missoulian*, Nov. 29, 1931, p. 8, c. 6.

56. "Ex-Bobcat Stars Smother Eagles," *The Daily Missoulian*, Dec. 26, 1931, p. 6, c. 8.

57. "High School Play Is Presented by Polson Students," *The Daily Missoulian*, Mar. 10, 1932, p. 9, c. 1.

58. "Bridge Dinner at Cline Home Is Enjoyable," *The Daily Missoulian*, Mar. 20, 1932, ed. sec., p. 6, c. 1-2.

59. "Polson Independents Whip Somers; Tackle Idle Hour Saturday," *The Daily Missoulian*, Dec. 8, 1932, p. 6, c. 6-7.

60. Ray T. Rocene, "Sport Jabs," *The Daily Missoulian*, Dec. 27, 1932, p. 6, c. 2-4.

61. Ray T. Rocene, "Sport Jabs," *The Daily Missoulian*, Jan. 6, 1933, p. 3, c. 2-3; Ray T. Rocene, "Sport Jabs," *The Daily Missoulian*, Feb. 5, 1933, p. 6, c. 2-3.

62. Ray T. Rocene, "Sport Jabs," *The Daily Missoulian*, Feb. 5, 1933, p. 6, c. 2-3; "Polson Wins from Plains Club, 58-30," *The Daily Missoulian*, Feb. 9, 1933, p. 5, c. 1.

63. "Polson Wins From Alberton Bearcats," *The Daily Missoulian*, Feb. 23, 1933, p. 6, c. 1.

64. "Polson Defeats Daily Quintette In Hoop Thriller," *The Daily Missoulian*, Feb. 27, 1933, p. 6, c. 5; "Bearded Magic Baffles Montana As Davids Triumph," *The Daily Missoulian*, Feb. 28, 1933, p. 5, c. 1.

65. "University Squad Plays Double-Header Here Friday," *The Daily Missoulian*, Dec. 13, 1934, p. 3, c. 1; Ray T. Rocene, "Sport Jabs," *The Daily Missoulian*, Feb. 26, 1935, p. 5, c. 1-2.

66. "Polson Team to Meet Kalispell," *The Daily Missoulian*, Dec. 26, 1935, p. 6, c. 1; "Polson Five Beats Standard Oil Team of Kalispell, 48-39" [sic], *The Daily Missoulian*, Dec. 27, 1935, p. 6, c. 7.

67. "Alberton Defeated by Polson's Quint," *The Daily Missoulian*, Jan. 12, 1936, p. 5, c. 3.

68. "Independents to Start Season," *The Daily Missoulian*, Dec. 4, 1936, p. 8, c. 3.

69. "University Team Opens Hoop Fray on Friday Night," *The Daily Missoulian*, Dec. 6, 1936, p. 6, c. 6; Ray T. Rocene, "Sport Jabs," *The Daily Missoulian*, Dec. 10, 1936, p. 7, c. 2-4.

70. "Good Shooting, Passing Bring Grizzlies Easy Victory," *The Daily Missoulian*, Dec. 12, 1936, p. 8, c. 1.

71. "Fast Dixon Agency Tossers Win Ninth Straight on Court," *The Daily Missoulian*, Jan. 22, 1940, p. 5, c. 8.

72. "Tournament Title Struggle Will Continue Here Today," *The Daily Missoulian*, Jan. 28, 1940, p. 6, c. 1-2.

73. "Flathead Indians to Elect Delegates to Organization for New Self Government," *The Daily Missoulian*, Dec. 9, 1935, p. 5, c. 1-2; "'Radicals' Beaten at Tribe Polls," *The Daily Missoulian*, Dec. 16, 1935, p. 1, c. 3, and p. 2, c. 6.

74. "Dixon," *The Daily Missoulian*, Jan. 14, 1937, p. 6, c. 2; "Hunting Party Home with Game," *The Daily Missoulian*, Oct. 9, 1937, p. 3, c. 8.

75. See for example: "Employees of Government Have Picnic," *The Daily Missoulian*, June 21, 1936, ed. sec., p. 4, c. 2; "St. Ignatius Girls' Hoop Team Honored," *The Daily Missoulian*, Mar. 13, 1938, ed. sec., p. 4, c. 8; "Parties Given for Departing Dixon Couple," *The Daily Missoulian*, May 8, 1938, ed. sec., p. 4, c. 7; "Benefit Dance," *The Daily Missoulian*, Jan. 10, 1941, p. 6, c. 2.

76. "Flathead Men Win Golf Play Sunday," *The Daily Missoulian*, Sept. 21, 1937, p. 6, c. 3; "Reservation Golf Club Holds Meet," *The Daily Missoulian*, Apr. 8, 1942, p. 6, c. 7.

77. "Phillip A. Roullier," *The Daily Missoulian*, June 16, 1955, p. 11, c. 5.

78. "Dixon," *The Daily Missoulian*, Oct. 23, 1936, p. 9, c. 5.

79. "Information About Service Men," *The Daily Missoulian*, June 11, 1944, p. 6, c. 4; "Phil Roullier Dies," *Hot Springs Sentinel*, June 16, 1955, p. 1, c. 6-7.

80. "Phil Roullier Dies," *Hot Springs Sentinel*, June 16, 1955, p. 1, c. 6-7; "Jim Thorpe, Indian Athlete, Visits Flathead on Return to California," *The Daily Missoulian*, July 23, 1949, p. 7, c. 2-3.

81. "Phil Roullier Dies," *Hot Springs Sentinel*, June 16, 1955, p. 1, c. 6-7; "Travel Division Plan Approved," *The Daily Missoulian*, Dec. 9, 1950, p. 3, c. 5.

82. "Phil Roullier Dies," *Hot Springs Sentinel*, June 16, 1955, p. 1, c. 6-7; "Large Crowd Attends Roullier Funeral," *Hot Springs Sentinel*, June 23, 1955, p, 1. c. 3.

83. "Alexander 'Sam' Clairmont," *Missoulian*, Mar. 26, 1992, p. B3, c. 1-2; "Ashley Funeral Services Held at St. Ignatius," *The Daily Missoulian*, Oct. 4, 1931, p. 10, c. 8.

84. "'Radicals' Beaten at Tribe Polls," *The Daily Missoulian*, Dec. 16, 1935, p. 1, c. 3, and p. 2, c. 6.

85. "Final Banquet Plans Will Be Made Tonight," *The Daily Missoulian*, Mar. 15, 1939, p. 6, c. 2; "John Dishman Is Made Head of Lake Sportsmen," *The Daily Missoulian*, Mar. 17, 1940, p. 6, c. 5; "W. C. Boettcher Is President of Lake Sportsmen," *The Daily Missoulian*, June 17, 1942, p. 8. c. 1.

86. "Board of Trustees to Be Reorganized," *The Daily Missoulian*, Apr. 11, 1952, p. 13, c. 3.

87. "Whites Betrayed Chief Charlo, Indian Testifies," *The Daily Missoulian*, Oct. 31, 1952, p. 1, c. 5, and p. 3, c. 2.

88. "Clairmont to Head Dixon P-TA," *The Daily Missoulian*, Sept. 26, 1958, p. 9, c. 3.

89. "Alexander 'Sam' Clairmont," *Missoulian*, Mar. 26, 1992, p. B3, c. 1-2.

Chapter 6
Archie McDonald: Haskell Institute and Montana Grizzly Football Star, 1930–1939

Archibald T. "Archie" McDonald, born on October 30, 1913, was the oldest child of Angus Pierre McDonald and Anne Hove McDonald. He had two brothers, Angus Predue, and Thomas Ranald, and one sister, Margaret Erin. He grew up to be a star football player for Haskell Institute in Lawrence, Kansas, and Montana State University in Missoula in the 1930s. He was a World War II veteran, rancher, and Confederated Salish and Kootenai Tribes tribal council member during a career that spanned forty years.[1]

Haskell Institute, 1930–1935

Archie McDonald was only 17 years old and still a high school student in 1930, but he played tackle on the Haskell junior varsity football team.[2] On September 19, 1930, the Haskell Reserve, the junior varsity with McDonald as a member, played a tie game against the State Teachers of Maryville, Missouri.[3] He also played on an intermural team in competition with other Haskell students in 1930.[4]

By the 1932 football season, Archie McDonald had made it to the Haskell varsity team where he played as a left guard. The team played 8 games in 1932 but won only 2. They lost 5 games and tied one.

The Haskell team opened the season on September 23, 1932, with a 12 to 6 victory over Ottawa University at Haskell before a crowd of 3,000 people.[5] But a week later, on October 1, 1932, Haskell lost an away game to Creighton University, 0 to 6. McDonald played right guard in this game.[6] Haskell lost to Notre Dame on October 8, 1932, at South Bend, Indiana, 0 to 73. According to the Haskell student newspaper, "Although completely outclassed, the Haskell boys gave everything they had and were in the game fighting from the start to the end, but could not stop the point manufacturing of the famed Irishmen."[7] McDonald was still a high school student at the time he played Notre Dame.

The Haskell team was able to beat Baker University on October 14, 1932, 25 to 0. The game was played at Haskell before a crowd of 2,000.[8] However, the Haskell team lost their game with Washburn College a week later on October 21, 1932. The score was Haskell 6 and Washburn 7 and the game had 4,000 spectators.[9] The Haskell team managed to tie Temple University at 14 points on November 4, 1932. This game was played before a crowd of 18,000 spectators at the Temple stadium.[10]

From there it was all downhill as Haskell lost the last two games of the 1932 season. St. Louis University beat Haskell in St. Louis 20 to 7 on November 11, 1932.[11] The final 1932 game was on Thanksgiving Day, November 24, 1932, against Xavier University in Cincinnati, Ohio. Xavier won 20 to 7. The Xavier game was hampered by a muddy field.[12]

Archie McDonald was among the 1932 players who lettered in football and were honored at a February 24, 1933, celebration.[13] On March 17, 1933, McDonald gave a talk at a St. Patrick's Day assembly on the retirement of coach William H. Dietz.[14] March 1933 also saw the start of the spring football season at Haskell. McDonald was one of the returning players from the 1932 team.[15] In June 1933, Archie McDonald graduated from the high school course at Haskell.[16]

The 1933 football season was not very successful. Haskell won only two games out of the nine played. They lost four games and had 3 scoreless ties. Archie McDonald was one of the twelve lettermen who turned out for the 1933 season. He was picked as right guard in the first-string lineup.[17] On September 22, 1933, the Haskell team had a scrimmage before their first game against St. Benedicts College.[18]

In the first game of the season, Haskell beat St. Benedicts College 25 to 0 on September 22, 1933.[19] Haskell continued winning by beating Washburn College on September 29, 1933, 6 to 0.[20]

Unfortunately, the rest of the 1933 season was not as successful. On October 7, 1933, Haskell played a scoreless tie against Creighton in the Creighton stadium. The Haskell players got close to scoring a touchdown four times, but "the Indians lacked the punch to put it over the last chalk line all through the game."[21] Haskell celebrated their football team with a big chicken feed on October 9, 1933.[22]

A few days later, on October 13, 1933, the Haskell team lost 0 to 31 to Temple University in a game played in Philadelphia.[23] Haskell had another scoreless tie on October 20, 1933, against Kansas State Teachers College in a game played at Haskell: "the best the Haskell team could do was to get within the 10-yard marker twice."[24] Remarkably, Haskell had yet another scoreless tie in their November 11, 1933, game against Grinnell College played at Haskell. According to the student newspaper, "Outgained by the Indians in every department of play and threatened on four occasions, the [Grinnell] Pioneers outrushed and outcharged [sic] the [Haskell] Braves when the ball was placed deep in their territory."[25]

Haskell then lost the last three games of their 1933 season. On November 18, 1933, Wichita University beat Haskell 28 to 6. Haskell was ahead at the end of the first half, but Wichita made a powerful comeback in the second half.[26] Haskell lost their game against Xavier played in Cincinnati, Ohio, on November 23, 1933, 13 to 24. The Haskell team scored the first touchdown in the game, but could not blunt the Xavier response.[27] Finally, Haskell lost to Tampa University 0 to 7 on Christmas Day 1933 in a game played in Florida.[28] Despite the losses, Haskell held a party for the football team on November 25, 1933. A luncheon was accompanied by dancing to a six-piece orchestra.[29]

In April 1934, Archie McDonald was awarded another letter in football. On May 23, 1934, he was elected sergeant-at-arms of the lettermen's club and gave a short talk.[30] During the 1934 commencement week, McDonald received athletic honors in football.[31]

Haskell played ten football games in 1934. They won three games, lost six, and tied one. Archie McDonald played right tackle.[32]

Their first game, against Washburn college, was played in Topeka, Kansas, on September 21, 1934, and resulted in a scoreless tie. Six thousand fans watched the game.[33] On September 28, 1934, Haskell lost the game they played in Emporia, Kansas, 0 to 6. The field was "a quagmire of mud." The winners were the Kansas State Teacher's College team.[34]

Haskell's first win was on October 6, 1934, against Creighton university at Omaha. The score was 7 to 6.[35] Then on October 12, 1934, Haskell lost their game against the Oklahoma Agriculture and Mechanical college played at Stillwater, Oklahoma, 6 to 9. The Haskell team started with a lead, but lost in the end to a field goal.[36] Then on October 19, 1934, Haskell suffered a 0 to 67 wipeout by the Duquesne university team.[37]

Haskell won their October 27, 1934, game against Grinnell college, 3 to 0, at Grinnell, Iowa. Haskell's George Summers scored a field goal.[38] The Haskell team went on to lose to Drake on November 3, 1934, in Des Moines, Iowa, 7 to 20. The game was played before a crowd of "2,000 rain soaked fans."[39] But Haskell bounced back on November 12, 1934, to win against the University of South Dakota at the Haskell homecoming and golden anniversary celebration. The score was 13 to 7.[40]

After the homecoming win, Haskell lost the final two games of the season. On November 24, 1934, they lost to Roanoke 0 to 13 at Roanoke, Virginia.[41] Haskell's final 1934 defeat was against Xavier university, on November 29, 1934. After an initial lead, Haskell lost, 6 to 38. The game was played at Cincinnati, Ohio.[42]

Archie McDonald lettered again in football. He received his award at the May 1934 Haskell commencement ceremony.[43]

During the off season from football, McDonald played inter-mural basketball. In January 1933, he played with a team called the "Hot Cha Club."[44] In 1934, Archie McDonald played center and was the leading scorer for the Sleeping Bears inter-mural basketball team.[45]

McDonald also dabbled in boxing.[46] He was a private in Company D of the 137th Infantry of the Haskell National Guard unit during the summer of 1932.[47] In 1934, McDonald won a boxing championship at the summer national guard camp at Fort Riley, Kansas.[48]

Montana State University, Missoula, 1936–1939

Archie McDonald enrolled as a student at Montana State University in Missoula during the 1935–1936 school year. In October 1935 he pledged to the Signa Nu fraternity. That same month he was selected as a referee for the interfraternity football competition.[49] He spent the summer of 1936 working on his father's Nirada ranch on the reservation, before returning to Missoula for the 1936–1937 school year.[50]

McDonald made it on the Grizzly football team in the fall of 1936 as a tackle but was on the second string. Leonard Noyes of Butte got the first-string position as left tackle and McDonald was the alternate.[51] McDonald was six feet two inches tall and weighed in at 207 pounds.[52]

In 1936 the Grizzlies played nine games. They won six and lost three. They lost the first two games to Washington State and the University of California at Los Angeles. Then they beat Idaho, Southern Branch; Gonzaga; and Montana State College before losing to Oregon State. They finished the season with wins against Idaho, San Francisco University, and North Dakota.[53]

McDonald substituted for Leonard Noyes as left tackle during the October 24, 1936, game against the Montana State College Bobcats played in Butte.[54] He traveled with the Grizzlies to Corvallis, Oregon, for the losing game against Oregon State at the end of October 1936.[55]

He played during a scrimmage on November 11, 1936, after several of his teammates suffered injuries.[56] McDonald substituted as tackle three days later on November 14, 1936, when the Grizzlies beat the Idaho Vandals 16 to 0 in a game played at Missoula.[57]

McDonald substituted for Noyes as left tackle on November 21, 1936, in the Grizzlies' 24 to 7 win over San Francisco University. That game was played before 5,500 spectators in Butte.[58] He was also an alternate for the November 26, 1936, game against North Dakota played in Missoula. The Grizzlies won that game 13 to 6 on Thanksgiving Day.[59]

On April 22, 1937, McDonald played tackle in a spring scrimmage game.[60] A few days later on April 27, 1937, McDonald was initiated into the M Club of Grizzly athletes.[61] He played in another scrimmage on May 1, 1937.[62]

The 1937 football season was to be a triumph for the Grizzlies. They played eight games and lost only to Idaho 0 to 6. McDonald was still alternate to Leonard Noyes as left tackle.[63] Noyes had been injured in an automobile accident during the summer of 1937, but he recovered enough to resume his place as first string left tackle when the season started September 25, 1937.[64]

On September 28, 1937, McDonald left with the Grizzlies for Texas to play the Texas Tech team. The Grizzlies won that game 13 to 6 on October 2, 1937.[65] McDonald was alternate left tackle in October 10, 1937, when the Grizzlies beat Oklahoma City. That game was played before 6,600 spectators in Great Falls, Montana.[66]

The Grizzlies played San Francisco University in Butte on October 16, 1937. The Grizzlies won 13 to 7. According to a newspaper report just before the game, "Archie has been showing lots of punch this week in scrimmage."[67] McDonald was still an alternate on October 30, 1937, when the Grizzlies beat the Montana State College Bobcats in Butte 19 to 0.[68]

On November 6, 1937, the Grizzlies played the Gonzaga Bulldogs in Missoula, The Grizzlies won 23 to 0. The Montana

Top: Archie McDonald, detail from 1937 Grizzly football team,
McKay photo, 94-2363, Toole Archives, Mansfield Library,
University of Montana, Missoula.
Bottom: Archie McDonald, *Sentinel* (Missoula: Associated
Students of Montana, State University at Missoula, 1938),p. 91.

State University student newspaper had predicted that McDonald and the other tackles would play a large part in the game against Gonzaga: "The tackle division of the Grizzly squad is one of the few not riddled by injuries."[69]

The Grizzlies were confident of victory over the Idaho Vandals in Moscow, Idaho, on November 20, 1937. The Montana coach switched McDonald from tackle to alternate guard "to strengthen the line against the line-plunging Vandals." The Moscow football field was wet from a steady rain during the game. Unfortunately for the Grizzlies, the Idaho team won the game 6 to 0, the Grizzlies' only loss during the 1937 season.[70]

In the November 25, 1937, Thanksgiving Day game against the North Dakota Sioux, North Dakota had a 3 to 0 lead at the end of the third quarter. The tide changed during the fourth quarter when, "Two alternate tackles, Harry Schaffer and Archie McDonald, sparked Montana's last half drive for a 14-3 triumph over North Dakota." This was the last game of the season for the 1937 Grizzlies.[71]

McDonald was one of five seniors in the 1937 team. On December 8, 1937, he won another letter M for football.[72] For a couple of months between January and March 1938 it looked like McDonald was eligible to play another year for the Grizzlies because Haskell was a junior college when he had played football in Kansas. However, in March 1938 the conference ruled him ineligible for 1938.[73]

During 1938, McDonald worked as an assistant coach during the Grizzlies' spring scrimmage.[74] At one point, McDonald was expected to play for the Grizzlies in 1939, but that possibility ended in January 1939.[75] On March 11, 1939, McDonald refereed a local boxing match at Lonepine on the Flathead Reservation.[76]

Archie McDonald's finale as a Montana State University Grizzly was in two games by a Grizzly alumni team during the spring of 1939. McDonald was part of the Golden Grizzly alumni team that beat the 1939 Montana State University varsity team 31 to 0 on May 10, 1939. On May 30, 1939, the Golden

Grizzly team beat the Montana State College Bobcat varsity team at Missoula 67 to 7.[77]

The spring 1939 alumni games rounded out McDonald's years as a Montana State University Grizzly, but he did play some pro-football in 1939 and 1940. He was a lineman for the Los Angeles Bulldogs and Pacific Coast All-Stars before World War II broke out.[78]

The 1937 football team was widely celebrated as one of the best Grizzly teams of all time. In 1955 it was considered one of the five major football teams in the nation.[79] On the twentieth anniversary of the 1937–1938 school year, McDonald attended a sportsmen's award dinner in Missoula honoring a coach from the 1937 team. The dinner was sponsored by the Missoula Chamber of Commerce on May 27, 1958.[80] In 1963, the silver anniversary of the 1938 season, McDonald attended a special celebration of the "Silver Grizzlies" in Missoula.[81]

World War II and Later Life

During the first years of World War II, Archie McDonald worked in war industries in Seattle. While in Seattle, he also played in the Seattle War Industry Football League in 1942.[82] In 1944 he was in the Army engineers and saw service in Okinawa and the South Pacific.[83]

In 1951 McDonald married Dorothy Schumer and between 1952 and 1958 they had five daughters: Anne, Marguerite, Katherine, Christine, and Mary. Mary died as an infant.[84] Archie boasted that he was the "proud papa of four cheer-leaders."[85]

In November 1955, the McDonalds moved from St. Ignatius to the McDonald family ranch in Niarada.[86] McDonald ran a herd of registered Hereford cattle. In 1960, he paid $2,480 for four head at a Missoula sale.[87]

He ran a modern and progressive cattle ranch, experimenting with fertilizers, breeding, and scheduling to improve the ranch operations and production.[88] During the late 1960s, he consigned animals to prominent Missoula Hereford cattle sales.[89] In 1964 he was elected as one of the Sanders County represen-

Archie McDonald, U.S. Army, World War II.
Courtesy Confederated Salish and Kootenai Tribes, Tribal
Council, Pablo, Montana.

tatives on the Western Montana Stockmen's Association.[90] Three years later in 1967, McDonald was elected as a director of the Missoula Hereford Association.[91]

Archie McDonald was a prominent community leader in the Hot Springs area. In 1963 and 1964, he served on the Hot Spring School District board.[92]

Between 1967 and his death in 1970, he was a member of the Confederated Salish and Kootenai Tribes tribal council.[93] He opposed the young activists and Red Power Movement in 1969, but also opposed a council resolution to eject VISTA volunteers from the reservation.[94]

McDonald had health problems in his later years. In 1960 he spent time in the Kalispell General Hospital. He was "gravely ill" in 1969 and confined to a wheel chair.[95] He died on September 12, 1970, of cancer at his Niarada ranch at the age of 57.[96]

Endnotes

1. "Angus Pierre McDonald," and "Archibald T. McDonald," Eugene Mark Felsman, Confederated Salish and Kootenai Tribes family group sheets, McNickle Library, Salish Kootenai College, Pablo, Montana.

2. *The Indian Leader* (Haskell Institute, Lawrence, Kansas), Sept. 12, 1930, p. 4.

3. "Haskell Reserves in Tie," *The Indian Leader*, Sept. 26, 1930, p. 6.

4. "Runners-Up, Gym Rats," *The Indian Leader*, Dec. 5, 1930, p. 5.

5. "Haskell Defeated Ottawa," *The Indian Leader*, Sept. 30, 1932, pp. 4-5.

6. "Haskell Bows to Creighton," *The Indian Leader*, Oct. 7, 1932, p. 7.

7. "The Irish Humble the Indians," *The Indian Leader*, Oct. 14, 1932, p. 6.

8. "Indians Romp to Goal," *The Indian Leader*, Oct. 21, 1932, p. 6.

9. "Haskell Is Defeated on Home Soil," *The Indian Leader*, Oct. 28, 1932, p. 4.

10. "Indians in a Tie Game," *The Indian Leader*, Nov. 11, 1932, p. 6.

11. "Haskell Defeated by St. Louis University," *The Indian Leader*, Nov. 18, 1932, p. 6.

12. "Haskell Loses Final Game," *The Indian Leader*, Nov. 25, 1932, p. 8; "Football Season is Over at Haskell," *The Indian Leader*, Dec. 2, 1932, p. 4.

13. "Varsity Football Squad Men Entertained," *The Indian Leader*, Mar. 3, 1933, p. 6; "Osceola Hall Notes," *The Indian Leader*, Mar. 24, 1933, p. 4.

14. "All School Assembly on St. Patrick's Day," *The Indian Leader*, Mar. 24, 1933, pp. 4-5.

15. "Spring Practice Is Underway," *The Indian Leader*, Mar. 24, 1933, pp. 6-7.

16. "Roster of Graduates," *The Indian Leader*, June 2, 9, 1933, pp. 6-11.

17. "Haskell Football Candidates in First Drill," *The Indian Leader*, Sept. 8, 1933, pp. 4-5; "Football at Haskell," *The Indian Leader*, Sept. 15, 1933, p. 5.

18. "Football at Haskell," *The Indian Leader*, Sept. 22, 1933, p. 6.

19. "Haskell Overwhelms St. Benedicts," *The Indian Leader*, Sept. 29, 1933, pp. 5-6.

20. "Haskell Downs Washburn," *The Indian Leader*, Oct. 6, 1933, pp. 3-4.

21. "Haskell-Creighton Game to a Scoreless Tie," *The Indian Leader*, Oct. 13, 1933, pp. 4-5.

22. "Football Night," *The Indian Leader*, Oct. 13, 1933, p. 6.

23. "Indians Meet Defeat in East," *The Indian Leader*, Oct. 20, 1933, p. 5.

24. "Indians and Hornets Play to a Scoreless Tie," *The Indian Leader*, Oct. 27, 1933, pp. 6-7.

25. "Haskell-Grinnell In a Scoreless Tie," *The Indian Leader*, Nov. 17, 1933, pp. 6-7.

26. "Haskell Downed by Wichita," *The Indian Leader*, Nov. 24, 1933, p. 4.

27. "Xavier Triumphs Over Haskell in Annual Clash," *The Indian Leader*, Dec. 8, 1933, pp. 5-6.

28. "Dabblings from the Gridiron and Court," *The Indian Leader*, Dec. 22, 1933, p. 4; "Notes of the Florida Trip That May Interest You," *The Indian Leader*, Jan. 5, 1934, pp. 4-5.

29. "Haskell Lettermen Entertained," *The Indian Leader*, Dec. 1, 1933, p. 4.

30. "Athletes to Receive Letters," *The Indian Leader*, Apr. 20, 1934, p. 9; "Annual 'H' Club Initiation," *The Indian Leader*, June 1, 1934, p. 4.

31. Retha E. Breeze, "Commencement Week: Resume of Haskell's 1934 Closing Exercises," *The Indian Leader*, June 8, 1934, pp. 5-8.

32. "Shorts from Local Sports," *The Indian Leader*, Sept. 21, 1934, p. 5.

33. "Haskell and Washburn in a Deadlock," *The Indian Leader*, Sept. 28, 1934, p. 6.

34. "First Loss of Season for Indians," *The Indian Leader*, Oct. 5, 1934, p. 8.

35. "Haskell Registers First Win," *The Indian Leader*, Oct. 12, 1934, p. 6.

36. "Haskell Lead Fades Late in Game," *The Indian Leader*, Oct. 19, 1934, p. 8.

37. "Duquesne Crushes Haskell," *The Indian Leader*, Oct. 26, 1934, p. 6.

38. "Haskell Wins on a Field Goal," *The Indian Leader*, Nov. 2, 1934, pp. 7-8.

39. "Haskell Loses to Drake in Rain," *The Indian Leader*, Nov. 9, 1934, pp. 3-4.

40. "Haskell Wins Homecoming Game," *The Indian Leader*, Nov. 23, 1934, pp. 25-27.

41. "Haskell Lacks Scoring Punch," *The Indian Leader*, Nov. 30, 1934, p. 6.

42. "Haskell Ends Season in Defeat," *The Indian Leader*, Dec. 7, 1934, p. 7.

43. "Shorts from Local Sports," *The Indian Leader*, Jan. 18, 1935, p. 6; Retha E. Breeze, "Commencement at Haskell – 1935," *The Indian Leader*, May 24, 1935, pp. 5-9.

44. "Boys Pick-Up Basket-Ball Tournament," *The Indian Leader*, Jan. 13, 1933, p. 7.

45. "Osceola-Keokuk League," *The Indian Leader*, Feb. 9, 1934, p. 9; "Sitting Bulls Defeat Sleeping Bears," *The Indian Leader*, Mar. 9, 1934, p. 6.

46. "News from Osceola Hall," *The Indian Leader*, Mar. 9, 1934, pp. 3-4.

47. "Haskell Military Organization Won Distinction at Camp Witside," *The Indian Leader*, Sept. 9, 1932, p. 5.

48. "Osceola Hall," *The Indian Leader*, Sept. 7, 1934, p. 4.

49. "Society," *The Montana Kaimin* (Montana State University, Missoula), Oct. 25, 1935, p. 2, c. 5-7; "Houses Start 1935 Touch Schedule with Two Games," *The Montana Kaimin*, Oct. 11, 1935, p. 4, c. 2.

50. Ray T. Rocene, "Sport Jabs," *The Daily Missoulian*, July 10, 1936, p. 10, c. 2-3.

51. "Call to Football for Scholastics and Grizzlies," *The Daily Missoulian*, Aug. 30, 1936, p. 7, c. 1; "Mobilization of Grizzly Football Battalion to Start," *The Daily Missoulian*, Sept. 9, 1936, p. 6, c. 1.

52. "Practice Battle Will Bring Out Grizzly Talent," *The Daily Missoulian*, Sept. 20, 1936, p. 6, c. 8.

53. Bob Gilluly, *The Grizzly Gridiron* (Missoula: Montana State University Press, 1960), pp. 102-103.

54. "Grizzlies Overwhelm Bobcats 27-0; Popovich Stars for University," *The Montana Kaimin*, Oct. 27, 1936, p. 3, c. 1-2.

55. "Grizzlies Set to Win Over Tough Beavers in Tomorrow's Clash," *The Montana Kaimin*, Oct. 30, 1936, p. 3, c. 1-3.

56. "Jinx Strikes at Cosgrove in Hot Grid Scrimmage," *The Daily Missoulian*, Nov. 12, 1936, p, 9, c. 2.

57. "Fighting Grizzlies Whip Vandals," *The Daily Missoulian*, Nov. 15, 1936, p. 11, c. 7-8, and p. 12, c. 4-6.

58. Ray T. Rocene, "Grizzlies Run Wild to Beat Dons," *The Daily Missoulian*, Nov. 22, 1936, p. 11, c. 7-8, and p. 12, c. 4-6.

59. "Brilliant Victory Over Sioux Climaxes Successful Season," *The Montana Kaimin*, Dec. 1, 1936, p. 3, c. 1-2.

60. "Vigorous Contact Drill on Gridiron," *The Daily Missoulian*, Apr. 22, 1937, p. 8, c. 5.

61. "M Club Initiates Eighteen Members," *The Montana Kaimin*, Apr. 30, 1937, p. 3, c. 3.

62. "Long Toss Earns University Reds a Grid Victory," *The Daily Missoulian*, May 2, 1937, p. 9, c. 6.

63. Gilluly, *The Grizzly Gridiron*, pp. 104-105.

64. "Whitman-Grizzly Night Clash Opens Season," *The Montana Kaimin*, Sept. 24, 1937, p. 1, c. 7-8, and p. 3, c. 3.

65. "Grizzly Squad Will Invade Raider's Lair," *The Montana Kaimin*, Sept. 28, 1937, p. 3, c. 3-4; Gilluly, *The Grizzly Gridiron*, pp. 104-105.

66. "Grizzly Herd Gallops Over Oklahoma Goldbugs," *The Montana Kaimin*, Oct. 12, 1937, p. 3, c. 1-3.

67. "Grizzlies Look for Speedy Play from Frisco Dons," *The Montana Kaimin*, Oct. 15, 1937, p. 3, c. 1-3; Gilluly, *The Grizzly Gridiron*, pp. 104-105.

68. "Undefeated Grizzlies Topple Stubborn Cats with Last-half Attack," *The Montana Kaimin*, Nov. 2, 1937, p. 3, c. 1-2, and p. 4, c. 2-3.

69. "Grizzlies Bid for National Fame Tomorrow," *The Montana Kaimin*, Nov. 5, 1937, p. 1, c. 7-8, and p. 4, c. 1; Gilluly, *The Grizzly Gridiron*, pp. 104-105.

70. "Montana Favored Over Strong Vandals," *The Montana Kaimin*, Nov. 19, 1937, p. 1, c. 7-8, and p. 4, c. 3-4; Gilluly, *The Grizzly Gridiron*, pp. 104-105.

71. "Grizzlies Rally to Topple Sioux," *The Daily Missoulian*, Nov. 26, 1937, p. 1, c. 7-8, and p. 11, c. 1-3; "Two Grizzly Scores During Last Quarter Defeat Nodaks 14-3," *The Montana Kaimin*, Nov. 30, 1937, p. 3, c. 1-3.

72. "Lazetich and Dolan Elected Co-captains for Next Season," *The Montana Kaimin,* Dec. 7, 1937, p. 3, c. 5-6; "Board Gives Twenty-eight Grid Awards," *The Montana Kaimin*, Dec. 10, 1937, p. 3, c. 7-8.

73. Ray T. Rocene, "Sport Jabs, *The Daily Missoulian*, Jan. 18, 1938, p. 6, c. 2-3; Ray T. Rocene, "Sport Jabs," *The Daily Missoulian*, Mar. 26, 1938, p. 6, c. 1-2.

74. Ray T. Rocene, "Sport Jabs," *The Daily Missoulian*, May 4, 1938, p. 7, c. 4-5.

75. Ray T. Rocene, "Sport Jabs," *The Daily Missoulian*, Nov. 27, 1938, p. 9, c. 2-5; Ray T. Rocene, "Sport Jabs," *The Daily Missoulian*, Jan. 26, 1939, p. 7, c. 3-4.

76. "Hot Springs Ring Performers Have Edge on Lonepine," *The Daily Missoulian,* Mar. 14, 1939, p. 6, c. 4.

77. "Golden Grizzly Eleven Dazzles Varsity 31 to 0," *The Daily Missoulian*, May 11, 1939, p. 1, c. 7, and p. 7, c. 2; "10 Touchdowns for Hot Golden Grizzlies: Cats Routed by 67-7 Score," *The Daily Missoulian*, May 31, 1939, p. 2, c. 5-7.

78. Ray T. Rocene, "Sport Jabs," *The Daily Missoulian*, Sept. 16, 1939, p. 6, c. 4-5; Ray T. Rocene, "Sport Jabs," *The Daily Missoulian*, Apr. 22, 1941, p. 6, c. 4-5.

79. Genell Jackson, "1937 Grizzlies Rated One of Five Major Football Teams in Nation," *The Montana Kaimin*, Sept. 30, 1955, p. 5, c. 1-2.

80. "Dinner May 27 to Feature Sports Awards," *The Daily Missoulian*, May 13, 1958, p. 8, c. 7.

81. L. T. Stidmon, "Grizzlies of 1936-1939 Will Be Honored," *The Montana Kaimin*, Oct. 11, 1963, p. 5, c. 1-5; Ray T. Rocene, "Rocene's Sport Jabs," *The Missoulian*, Oct. 13, 1963, p. 8, c. 1-2.

82. Ray T. Rocene, "Sport Jabs," *The Daily Missoulian*, Sept. 23, 1942, p. 8, c. 4-6.

83. "M'Donald in City," *The Daily Missoulian*, Jan. 19, 1945, p. 5, c. 3; Jim Crane, "McDonald: Rancher with Responsibilities," *The Missoulian*, June 9, 1968, p. 16, c. 1-8.

84. "Archibald T. McDonald," Eugene Mark Felsman, Confederated Salish and Kootenai Tribes family group sheets, McNickle Library, Salish Kootenai College, Pablo, Mont..

85. Ray T. Rocene, "Ray T. Rocene's Sport Jabs," *The Daily Missoulian*, Feb. 23, 1958, p. 11, c. 3-5.

86. "Honor McDonalds at Farewell Party," *The Daily Missoulian*, Nov. 6, 1955, p. 22, c. 7.

87. "Record Price Paid for Bull at Top Cut Show, Sale," *The Daily Missoulian*, Feb. 16, 1960, p. 1, c. 2-3, and p. 2, c. 6-8.

88. Jim Crane, "McDonald: Rancher with Responsibilities," *The Missoulian,* June 9, 1968, p. 16, c. 1-8.

89. "Top Cut Show and Sales," *The Missoulian*, Jan. 29, 1967, p. 18, c. 1-2; "20th Annual Top Cut Show and Sale," *The Missoulian*, Feb. 4, 1968, p. 54, c. 1-2.

90. John Rhone, "In Meeting at Hot Springs Stockmen Elect Tripp," *The Missoulian*, May 3, 1964, p. 18, c. 1-3.

91. "Hereford Group Told Business Is Now in 'Era of Measuring,'" *The Missoulian*, Feb. 14, 1967, p. 4, c. 3-4.

92. "15 Sanders County School Posts Open," *The Missoulian*, Mar. 8, 1963, p. 6, c. 2-3; "Hot Springs Looking To Its School Needs," *The Missoulian*, Feb. 7, 1964, p. 7, c. 1-2.

93. "One Incumbent Keeps Tribal Council Seat," *The Missoulian*, Dec. 17, 1967, p. 17, c. 7-8.

94. E. W. "Bill" Morigeau and Archie T. McDonald, "Not the Way," *The Missoulian*, June 3, 1969, p. 4, c. 5-8; Denn Curran, "Tribal Council Votes Against Reservation VISTA Program," *The Missoulian*, June 7, 1969, p. 7, c. 5-8.

95. "Hospital Patients," *The Daily Missoulian*, Jan. 15, 1960, p. 10, c. 4; "Keeping Up with Jones," *The Missoulian*, Sept. 26, 1969, p. 6, c. 7-8; "Keeping Up with Jones," *The Missoulian*, Oct. 16, 1969, p. 11, c. 7-8.

96. "Archie K. McDonald Dies at His Home," *The Missoulian*, Sept. 14, 1970, p. 1, c. 5-6; "Keeping Up with Jones," *The Missoulian*, Sept. 15, 1970, p. 10, c. 4-5.

Chapter 7
Marvin Camel:
Native American Two-Time
World Boxing Champion,
1962-1990

Marvin Camel was an outstanding athlete in a family noted for their hard work and athletic talent. He was the sixth child
of Henry William Camel, a Black man from North Carolina,
and Alice Nenemay Camel, a full blood Pend d'Oreille Indian
from the Flathead Indian Reservation. His parents met in Oregon during World War II and were married in Portland in 1943.
Marvin was born on December 24, 1950, in St. Ignatius on the
reservation, and he had twelve full brothers and sisters.[1] Marvin's father worked for years as a ranch hand on H. O. Bell's Bar
Lazy B ranch on the reservation. Bell was a prominent Missoula
businessman with many enterprises in western Montana in addition to the ranch. Henry worked hard, but the family was poor
and suffered from discrimination on the reservation.[2] According
to Joe McDonald, then the Ronan High School principal and
coach, "They were an in-between family. . . Because they were
part black, they didn't get involved in Indian things like powwows and drumming. But they weren't acquainted with black
[culture] either."[3]

Henry was an amateur boxer and coached local boys and
his children in the Desert Horse Boxing Club in Polson.[4] The
boxing skills and general athletic abilities of the Camel children
gave them status in high school despite being poor and part
Black. They were always supported and cared for by their mother
and siblings and went on to accomplished careers.[5] By 1973, just
before he turned professional, Marvin had 151 amateur bouts
over ten years with 125 wins and 26 losses.[6]

In 1968–1970, Marvin took a break from boxing to concentrate on football, basketball, and track for Ronan High School.[7] Joe McDonald recounted a Polson track meet when Marvin was a sophomore in high school. Marvin was severely spiked in the lower leg and a doctor was called to sew up the gash in his leg. Despite being cautioned to rest and heal, in a few minutes Marvin was running one leg of a mile relay.[8]

After high school, Marvin Camel returned to boxing, and in July 1971 Elmer Boyce, a Missoula businessman and boxing promoter, became his manager and employer. Camel moved to Missoula and Boyce gave him room and board and a job at Montana Music Rentals fixing pinball machines. For ten years, until 1981, Boyce arranged for professional fights for Camel.[9] Camel's professional boxing career ran from 1973 to 1990 and totaled 62 fights. He won 45 of them (21 by knockout), lost 13 (8 by knockout), and had four draws. In March 1980, Camel won the World Boxing Council World Cruiserweight Championship, and, in December 1983, he won the International Boxing Federation World Cruiserweight Championship. Camel's boxing took him around the world, with matches in Italy, Denmark, Canada, Germany, France, and Yugoslavia. Most of his matches were in Las Vegas, Nevada, but he also fought in Butte, Coeur d'Alene, California, and other cities. Some of the matches were in Missoula with a couple on the Flathead Reservation.[10]

Camel kept up a remarkable conditioning regimen in Missoula but had trouble getting sparring partners and opponents in western Montana. Missoula was isolated from most of the boxing world and some opponents had trouble adjusting to his left-handed fighting style.[11] In January 1972, Boyce sent Camel to Tacoma, Washington, to train with the Tacoma Boys' Club boxing team. At Tacoma he could get more sparring partners and fights than he could in Missoula.[12]

In June 1972, Camel was selected by the Montana Amateur Athletic Union as the outstanding male athlete in Montana.[13] In February 1973, he married Sherry Clairmont. Sherry was to give

Marvin Camel.
Courtesy Renee Camel, Pablo, Montana.

Camel several children and worked in her husband's corner as a second for many of his boxing matches.[14]

After a false start in April 1973 when his planned opponent suffered a broken nose in training and could not fight, Camel finally initiated his professional career on June 25, 1973, in Butte, Montana. Camel knocked down Joe Williamson three times in the first round. The referee stopped the fight, giving Camel a victory in his first professional bout.[15] Between January 1975 and April 1976, Camel had eleven fights against various opponents in Las Vegas.[16]

Camel took on Angel Oquendo, a New York boxer, in a ten-round fight on May 8, 1976, before a hometown crowd in Missoula. Camel won the match on a unanimous decision. After the fight, Camel commented on the presence of friends and relatives in the crowd: "They were on my side all the way and that helps," Camel said. "It psyches you up and gives you a little more energy."[17]

Two months later, however, Camel suffered his first loss as a professional. Matthew Saad Muhammad (also known as Matthew Franklin) took a split decision over Camel on July 17, 1976, in Stockton, California.[18] Camel reversed the loss to Saad Muhammad with a split decision victory in an October 23, 1976, rematch fought in Missoula. Unfortunately, that fight only attracted 854 spectators. Elmer Boyce the promoter for the fight, reportedly lost more than $15,000 that night.[19]

In between Camel's two encounters with Saad Muhammad, he fought Johnny Townsend twice. On August 28, 1976, he beat Townsend in Missoula, and on September 25, 1976, he defeated Townsend in Spokane, Washington.[20]

On May 6, 1977, Camel met Gary Summerhays in Missoula. Summerhays was the Canadian light heavyweight champion. Camel got a victory on a unanimous decision. After the fight Summerhays complimented Camel as "one of the best fighters I've fought."[21]

During a June 28, 1977, fight against Danny Brewer in Seattle, Camel lost after he suffered a gash above his left eye. Camel was ahead in the fight before it was stopped. The wound healed, but reoccurrences of the injury would plague Camel, for the rest of his boxing career.[22]

A really local fight for Camel was his August 20, 1977, battle against Ron Wilson at the Pony Palace between Ronan and Polson on the Flathead Reservation. The evening boxing card featured Montana boxers, including Marvin's younger brother Kenny Camel and his brother-in-law Richard Jansen. Despite being knocked down in the eighth round, Marvin Camel won a unanimous decision. A crowd of 2,500 spectators cheered on the local fighters.[23]

After several other fights around the country, Camel returned to the reservation on May 27, 1978, to fight Chuck Warfield at the high school gym in St. Ignatius. Camel scored a knockout in the fifth round.[24]

Camel got a knockout over Tom Bertha of New York in the second round on November 11, 1978. The Bertha fight was held in Missoula with 1,500 spectators.[25] According to Camel's promoter Elmer Boyce, only one of the many boxing matches he had arranged in Missoula over the years had made any money. Paid attendance in Missoula was too low.[26]

After winning two matches in Las Vegas, Camel fought David Smith of Los Angeles in Missoula on April 24, 1979. Despite suffering a reinjury over his left eye, Camel won this match with a technical knockout in the ninth round. There were some 3,000 paid spectators to the fight which delighted promoter Elmer Boyce: "It's the finest crowd we've ever had." Many of the fans came down from the Flathead Reservation. Victor Lumprey of Arlee said, "I just came to see Marvin fight." Abel Combs of the Jocko Valley added, "I just came to see Marvin win."[27]

Camel's next bout in Missoula was against Bill Sharkey of New York on June 5, 1979. Camel easily won a unanimous decision and Sharkey complained he couldn't "breath this mountain air." The first account was that there were 3,000 spectators. Boyce later corrected that, saying only 1,426 paid to attend the fight and he lost $21,000 on the night. He angrily retorted, "The Missoula people will never see Marvin Camel fight again."[28]

Camel's next two fights were in Nevada and Texas. Then Camel got a fight on December 8, 1979, in the resort town of Split, Yugoslavia, against Mate Parlov. Originally announced to take place in Monte Carlo, Monaco, the bout was moved to Parlov's hometown in Yugoslavia. The world championship of the World Boxing Council Cruiserweight Division was on the line.[29]

Many observers thought Camel won the fight with Parlov, but two of the three judges scored it as a draw. Camel fumed, "It's a robbery," and Parlov admitted that "If the match was held in the United States I would've lost." Even the Yugoslav news agency admitted that Camel should have been declared the winner.[30] The World Boxing Council upheld the decision of the officials calling the fight a draw.[31]

Later that month, Marvin and Sherry Camel had a second son in a Missoula hospital.[32] February 2, 1980, was declared Marvin Camel Day on the Flathead Reservation. A feast and powwow were held at the St. Ignatius Community Center in his honor. Michael Joseph, Doug Allard, and Walter McDonald gave speeches about Camel's accomplishments. Johnny Arlee, Confederated Salish and Kootenai Tribes cultural leader, and Michael Joseph presented Camel with a war staff made of bearskin with 39 eagle feathers commemorating his 39 professional fights.[33]

Camel got a re-match with Mate Parlov on March 31, 1980, in Las Vegas. Camel's fight was on the same card with the Larry Holmes and Leroy Jones heavyweight battle at Caesars Palace. Both Camel and Parlov were bleeding by the end of the fifteen rounds, but Camel won a unanimous decision. Camel had won the world championship in the World Boxing Council's Cruiserweight Division.[34]

A few days later, Camel arrived on the reservation to a series of welcome signs and a celebration at the St. Ignatius Community Center. The local Missoula newspaper ran a congratulatory editorial. On April 11, 1980, he was presented with the key to the city of his hometown in Ronan and the Montana Governor proclaimed the day as "Marvin Camel Day" in the state.[35]

Camel's title defense was delayed due to an eye injury he suffered while welding. Other reports say the eye injury was received while sparring.[36] Finally on November 25, 1980, Camel fought Carlos De Leon, a Puerto Rican, in New Orleans. Both fighters were bloodied by the end of the fight. Camel lost his title when two of the judges scored the bout in De Leon's favor.[37] A crowd of 1,000 fans watched the match on closed circuit television at the University of Montana Field House in Missoula.[38]

Camel and his manager, Elmer Boyce, feuded during much of 1981. In July 1981, Camel signed on with Fred Harbeck of Missoula as his new manager. Camel was not satisfied with Boyce's efforts to get him sparring partners and additional fights.[39]

Camel won four more fights in Billings and Nevada before he was able to get a rematch with Carlos De Leon on February 24, 1982, in Atlantic City, New Jersey. The only place in Montana that received the satellite transmission of the title rematch was at Phillipsburg.[40] Camel bled profusely during the fight and the referee stopped the battle in round eight. De Leon won by a technical knockout and kept the WBC Cruiserweight Championship.[41]

During the summer of 1982, Camel opened a restaurant-youth recreation center in Ronan. His brother, Bobby Camel, was the cook. Marvin had hopes of developing a gym and fitness center for area youth. He also wanted to start a pinball and electronic amusement game business to use the skills he learned during his years working for Elmer Boyce.[42] Unfortunately Camel's business closed after a few months. Camel later noted, "The food and video didn't work together."[43]

In the meantime, Camel fought Leo Rogers in Omaha on June 30, 1982. Camel won in four rounds.[44] In August 1982, his manager, Fred Harbeck, sold Camel's contract to the fighter himself. Camel considered going it alone and boxing as an independent fighter.[45] In the summer of 1983, Camel moved from Montana to Los Angeles, hoping to advance his boxing career. At

Los Angeles, he met and married his second wife, Norma Josey Camel.[46]

On December 13, 1983, Camel beat Roddy MacDonald in Halifax, Canada. The fight was marred by accusations that Camel had made a low blow in the fifth round. A day later MacDonald acknowledged that Camel had not thrown a low blow during the fight. The victory over MacDonald made Camel the International Boxing Federation Cruiserweight World Champion.[47]

Lee Roy Murphy was the top contender waiting to challenge Camel for the International Boxing Federation title. But Camel suffered a back injury in training and had to postpone fighting Murphy.[48]

Camel finally met Murphy on October 6, 1984, in Billings, Montana. Again, Camel lost on a technical knockout after fourteen rounds due to cuts over his eyes. Two of the judges had Camel ahead by four points before the fight was stopped. Camel insisted he could have finished the fight and complained to the Montana Board of Athletics. The board declined to hear Camel's complaint and Camel lost the International Boxing Federation Cruiserweight World Championship.[49]

Camel had no professional boxing matches in 1985. Between 1986 and 1988, he lost five fights and had one draw. The bouts were scattered around the world: Idaho, Italy, North Dakota, France, and Germany. In 1989, Camel fought four opponents in Great Falls, Butte, and Washington State. He won two of the 1989 fights, lost one, and had one draw. His final professional fight was on June 11, 1990, against Eddie Taylor in Minnesota. He lost that fight.[50]

When Camel retired from boxing in 1990, he was living in Los Angeles and needed to find a new line of work. He decided not to move back to the reservation: "There is really nothing calling me back. . . Being a two-time champion wasn't worth a hill of beans on the reservation."[51] In 1993, Camel moved to Florida to be near his second wife's family. Since then he has lived in central Florida but has occasionally visited his three sons, siblings, and friends on the Flathead Reservation.[52]

Endnotes

1. "Henry William Camel," Eugene Mark Felsman, Confederated Salish and Kootenai Tribes family group sheets, McNickle Library, Salish Kootenai College, Pablo, Mont.

2. Brian D'Ambrosio, *Warrior in the Ring: The Life of Marvin Camel, Native American World Champion Boxer* (Helena, Mont.: Riverbend Publishing, 2015), pp. 28-31.

3. Lauren Russel, "Family Legacy: Sports Shaped How Henry Camel's 18 Children Grew Up, But Left Different Imprints on Their Lives," in Karl Krempel and Carol Van Valkenburg, eds., "The Spirit of Sport: Recreation on Montana's Reservation" (The UM School of Journalism, Missoula, Mont., 2008), p. 35. Supplement to *Missoulian*, May 24, 2008.

4. D'Ambrosio, *Warrior in the Ring*, pp. 30-31.

5. Russel, "Family Legacy," pp. 33-34.

6. Hal Mathew, "Stallings Battles Lyle Tonight," *The Missoulian*, Apr. 14, 1973, p. 9, c. 1-5.

7. "Loyola, Polson Pace Offense," *The Missoulian*, Nov. 8, 1968, p. 15, c. 4-8; "Ronan Opens Against Eureka," *The Missoulian*, Nov. 28, 1968, p. 18, c. 5.

8. John Stromes, "Meet Ronan's Remarkable Camel Family," *Missoulian*, Dec. 7, 1979, p. 1, c. 1-8, and p. 23, c. 1-8.

9. D'Ambrosio, *Warrior in the Ring*, pp. 44-50.

10. "Marvin Camel," Boxrec.com, accessed Feb. 18, 2022.

11. Jeff Herman, "Portrait of a Middleweight," *The Missoulian*, Sept. 12, 1971, p. 10, c. 1-8; Don Brunell, "The Brighter Side," *The Missoulian*, Dec. 1, 1971, p. 10 c. 1-2.

12. Don Brunell, "The Brighter Side," *The Missoulian*, Jan. 23, 1972, p. 14, c. 1-2.

13. "Camel, Braunberger Receive AAU Awards," *The Missoulian*, June 19, 1972, p. 11, c. 6-8.

14. "Camel, Clairmont Are Wed," *The Missoulian*, Mar. 11, 1973, p. 38.

15. Hal Mathew, "Lyle Decisions Stallings," *The Missoulian*, Apr. 15, 1973, p. 11, c. 5-8; Hudson Willse, "Camel Turns Pro Tonight," *The Missoulian*, June 25, 1973, p. 12, c. 5-8; "Camel Wins," *The Missoulian*, June 26, 1973, p. 13, c. 4.

16. "Marvin Camel," Boxrec.com, accessed Feb. 18, 2022.

17. John Blanchette, "Camel Confuses Oquendo," *The Missoulian*, May 9, 1976, p. 13, c. 1-4.

18. "Camel Drops Split Decision," *The Missoulian*, July 19, 1976, p. 9, c. 1-2.

19. John Blanchette, "Camel's Split-Decision Stands," *The Missoulian*, Oct. 27, 1976, p. 13, c. 4-6; John Blanchette, "What 'ja Think?" *The Missoulian*, Oct. 27, 1976, p. 13, c. 7-8.

20. "Camel Brothers Win by Decision, Kayo," *The Missoulian*, Aug. 29, 1976, p. 17, c. 1-3; "Camel Decisions Townsend," *The Missoulian*, Sept. 28, 1976, p. 11, c. 5-6.

21. "Camel Controls 12-Rounder," *Missoulian*, May 7, 1977, p. 15, c. 5-8.

22. D'Ambrosio, *Warrior in the Ring*, pp. 82-83.

23. "Professional Boxing," *Missoulian*, Aug. 19, 1977, p. 16, c. 6-8; Dennis Jones, "Camel Earns Decision," *Missoulian*, Aug. 21, 1977, p. 15, c. 1-3.

24. Dennis Jones, "Camel Scores Kayo," *Missoulian*, May 28, 1978, p. 14, c. 4-5.

25. Daryl Gadbow, "Camel Defuses the Bomb with a Second-Round KO," *Missoulian*, Nov. 12, 1978, p. 19, c. 1-8.

26. Daryl Gadbow, "Camel's Manager May See Dream Come True," *Missoulian*, Apr. 11, 1979, p. 21, c. 4-8, and p. 25, c. 1-6.

27. "Camel Wins TKO," *Missoulian*, Apr. 25, 1979, p. 19, c. 1-8; John Stromnes, "'Parking Lot Armada' Follows Camel, Smith," *Missoulian*, Apr. 26, 1979, p. 17, c. 1-8.

28. Daryl Gadbow, "Camel Easily 'Cruises' Past Sharkey," *Missoulian*, June 6, 1979, p. 19, c. 1-8; Donna Syvertson, "Boyce Says 'No More' After $21,000 Loss," *Missoulian*, June 8, 1979, p. 7, c. 4-6.

29. "Camel's Title Bout: From Monte Carlo... to Split," *Missoulian*, Nov. 6, 1979, p. 7, c. 1-8.

30. "Camel Disgusted with Draw," *Missoulian*, Dec. 9, 1979, p. 23, c. 1-8; "Yugoslavian Press Says Camel a Victim of Officials," *Missoulian*, Dec. 10, 1979, p. 9, c. 1-8.

31. "WBC Upholds Camel Draw," *Missoulian*, Dec. 19, 1979, p. 17, c. 7-8.

32. "Births," *Missoulian*, Dec. 31, 1979, p. 2, c. 6.

33. Richard Eggert, "Tribes Honor Marvin Camel," *Missoulian*, Feb. 5, 1980, p. 13, c. 4-8.

34. Daryl Gadbow, "Camel, a Modest Champ, Is Making Modest Plans," *Missoulian*, Apr. 1, 1980, p. 1, c. 1-2, and p. 2, c. 1-3; Daryl Gadbow, "Camel Wins the World Title," *Missoulian*, Apr. 1, 1980, p. 5, c. 1-8, and p. 6, c. 3-4.

35. Daryl Gadbow, "Tribes Welcome Champion Home," *Missoulian*, Apr. 5, 1980, p. 7, c. 1-8; "Ticklers: A Man To Make Montana Proud," *Missoulian*, Apr. 6, 1980, p. 6, c. 1; "Camel Honored in Hometown Ronan," *Missoulian*, Apr. 12, 1980, p. 17, c. 2.

36. "Camel Fight Is Postponed," *Missoulian*, June 9, 1980, p. 13, c. 4-6; D'Ambrosio, *Warrior in the Ring*, pp. 118-119.

37. Daryl Gadbow, "Camel Loses Title," *Missoulian*, Nov. 26, 1980, p. 9, c. 1-2.

38. "Camel's Reign Ends," *Missoulian*, Nov. 27, 1980, p. 19, c. 1-8.

39. Daryl Gadbow, "Camel, Boyce Still Going Round," *Missoulian*, Apr. 4, 1981, p. 13, c. 1-8; "Camel Switches Managers," *Missoulian*, July 13, 1981, p. 13, c. 4-6.

40. Daryl Gadbow, "Philipsburg's Got All the Action for Fight Fans," *Missoulian*, Feb. 24, 1982, p. 15, c. 1-8.

41. Daryl Gadbow, "Cut Stops Camel," *Missoulian*, Feb. 25, 1982, p. 15, c. 4-6.

42. Daryl Gadbow, "Retirement Will Have to Wait for Marvin Camel," *Missoulian*, Mar. 24, 1982, p. 15, c. 1-6; Dennis Jones, "Marvin Camel Keeps His Irons in the Fire," *Missoulian*, Aug. 14, 1982, p. 5, c. 1-6.

43. D'Ambrosio, *Warrior in the Ring*, p. 155; Nick Gerarios, "Injury, Financial Woes Plague Camel," *Missoulian*, Apr. 26, 1984, p. 15, c. 1-8.

44. "Camel Stops Rogers in 4," *Missoulian*, July 2, 1982, p. 21, c. 1-6.

45. "Camel, Manager Part Company," *Missoulian*, Aug. 18, 1982, p. 13, c. 1-2.

46. D'Ambrosio, *Warrior in the Ring*, pp. 155-158.

47. "Camel Keeps the Title," *Missoulian*, Dec. 14, 1983, p. 17, c. 8; "Camel's Opponent Admits Kayo Punch Was Legal," *Missoulian*, Dec. 15, 1983, p. 23, c. 4-5.

48. Nick Geranios, "Injury, Financial Woes Plague Camel," *Missoulian*, Apr. 26, 1984, p. 15, c. 1-8.

49. Dave Trimmer, "Camel Loses IBF Crown," *Missoulian*, Oct. 7, 1984, p. 24, c. 7-8; Donna Syvertson, "State Board to Review Camel's Protest of Fight," *Missoulian*, Oct. 11, 1984, p. 15, c. 1-8; "State Board Won't Rule on Camel Protest," *Missoulian*, Oct. 13, 1984, p. 12, c. 5-6.

50. "Marvin Camel," Boxrec.com, accessed Feb. 18, 2022.

51. D'Ambrosio, *Warrior in the Ring*, pp. 179-182.

52. Ibid, pp. 198-205.

Index

A

acting 35, 59
Adams, Johnny 49
Alberton High School basketball
    team 54
Albright College football team 31
alcohol 24, 38, 49
Allard, Charles, Jr. 5–13
Allard, Doug 94
Allard, Emerence Brown 9
Allard, Louis Charles, Sr. 9
Allen, H. S. 29–30
American Red Cross 32
Anaconda Athletic Club football
    team 5–6
Anaconda High School basketball
    team 58
Arlee, Johnny 94

B

Baker University football team 74
basketball 31–32, 53–63, 77
Bell, H. O. 89
Bell, William V., Jr. 20
Ben West Colts football team 8
Berg, John 16
Bertha, Tom 93
Big Knife (Kootenai chief) 15
Billings Polytechnic Institute foot-
    ball team 59
Blodgett, Ashbury 23
Boettcher Hardware independent
    basketball team 62

Boettcher, W. C., Mr. and Mrs. 62
Bouldin, Clarence 19
boxing 45–49, 77, 89–97
Boyce, Elmer 90, 92–95
Brewer, Danny 92–93
Brigham Young University football
    team 60
Brotherhood of North American
    Indians 25
Bucknell College football team 31
Butte Business College football
    team 8
Butte Central High School basket-
    ball team 58
Butte High School football team 8

C

Calac, Pete 37–38
Camel, Alice Nenemay 89
Camel, Bobby 95
Camel, Henry William 89
Camel, Kenny 93
Camel, Marvin 89–100
Camel, Norma Josey 96
Camel, Sherry Clairmont 90, 92,
    94
Carlisle Indian School, Carlisle,
    Penna. 23, 29–32
Carroll College, Helena. *See* Mount
    St. Charles College, Helena
Charlo, Martin (Salish chief)
    24–25
cheerleader 31

Clairmont, Alexander "Sam"
    53–54, 56–63
Clairmont, Alphonse 53
Clairmont, Armine Morigeau 53
Clairmont, Sherry. *See* Camel,
    Sherry Clairmont
College of Emporia 34
College of Montana, Deer Lodge 5
Combs, Abel 93
Confederated Salish and Kootenai
    Tribes 65, 67
Corvallis independent basketball
    team 63
Cote, Ray "Tiger" 47-48
Coyle, Eddie 47
Cramer, Ben 19
Creighton University football team
    73–74, 76
Cunningham, Clarence 46
Curran, Jack 20, 22–24

D

Daily Company independent bas-
    ketball team 62
debating 32–33
De Leon, Carlos 95
Denison, Benjamin H. 10
Desert Horse Boxing Club 89
Dietz, William H. 74
Dishman, Orin 45
Dixon High School basketball team
    54
Dixon School Parent-Teacher Asso-
    ciation 67
Donaldson, Buster 49
Drake college football team 76
Dupuis, Ann Pablo 45
Dupuis, Jimmy 45–51
Dupuis, Orson Samuel 45
Duquesne University football team
    76

E

Egan, Kenneth 53–54, 57–61

F

Ferrell, George 6–7
Flathead Agency, Bureau of Indian
    Affairs 65, 67
Flathead Agency Independent
    basketball team 63
Flathead Business Committee 10
Flathead Tribal Council 10
football 5–9, 29–38, 59–60, 73–81
forestry 65
Fort Missoula football team 8
Fort Shaw Indian School football
    team 8
Fort Simco, White Swan, Washing-
    ton 65
Franklin, Matthew. *See* Muham-
    mad, Matthew Saad
Frenchtown High School basketball
    team 53

G

Golden Grizzly alumni football
    team 80–81
golf 65
Gonzaga college basketball team
    60
Gonzaga college football team 77,
    78
Gotch, Frank A. 15–16, 19
Gravelle, Abel "Two Feathers"
    15–20, 23
Gravelle, Cecille 23
Gravelle, Francois 15
Gravelle, Isabelle 15
Great Buffalo and Wild West Show
    9
Great Falls High School basketball
    team 58

Greenwood, Bob 38
Grenier, Mose 20
Grinnell College football team
        75–76
Gross, William 60
Gunnery Military Academy, Wash-
        ington, Conn. 5

H

Hamel, Howard 47
Harbeck, Fred 95
Haskell Indian Institute, Lawrence,
        Kan. 33–35, 73–77
Haugen Civilian Conservation
        Corps 63
Hays Normal College football team
        34
Helena Athletic Club football team
        5–6
Helena Eagles baketball team
        61–62
Hildrich, Dave 46
Holmes, Larry 94
Holy Name Society 32
horse racing 9
horseshoes 61
Hot Springs bathhouse 65
Hot Springs Chamber of Com-
        merce 65
Hutchin, Mr. 9

I

Indian Rights Association 33
injuries 6–7
International Boxing Federation
        World Cruiserweight Cham-
        pionship 90, 96
investments 10
Invincible Debating Society 32–33

J

Jackson Sundown 9–10
Jansen, Richard 93
Jones, Deane 45–46
Jones, Leroy 94
Joseph, Michael 94

K

Kalispell High School basketball
        team 57
Kallowat, Jim 30
Kansas Aggies 35
Kansas State Teachers College foot-
        ball team 75–76
Kansas University of Commerce
        football team 33
Kelley, Bruce 48
Knights of Columbus 32, 35

L

Lahood, Dixie 47
Lake County Sportsmen's Associa-
        tion 67
Lassa, Nick 3, 29–44
Lassa, Rose Sorrell 38
Lassaw 29
Lassaw, Louise 29
Lassaw, Nick, Jr. 38
Lassaw, Zella M. 38
Lebanon Valley College. 31
Leiback, Butch 49
Lingo, Walter 37
Linn, Cal "Branding Iron" 47
Long Time Sleep. See Lassa, Nick
Los Angeles Bulldogs football team
        81
Loyola High School basketball
        team 53–54
Lumprey, Victor 93

M

MacDonald, Roddy 96
Manhattan High School basketball
    team 58
Marquette University football team
    34
Marsh, Ole 19–20
Mary Michell 29
Matt, Alexander 24–25
Matt, Henry 20–25
Matt, Margaret St. Mark 24
Matt, Marguerite Pokerjim 25
Mattson, Carl 19
Matt, William 20, 22–24
McAuley, Jim 19
McCallum, Battling 48
McCallum, "Spider" 48
McDonald, Angus 19
McDonald, Anne 81
McDonald, Archibald T. "Archie"
    (1913-1970) 3, 73–88
McDonald, Archie Thomas (1896-
    1980) 2
McDonald, Christine 81
McDonald, Dorothy Schumer 81
McDonald, Duncan 10
McDonald, James "Bugs" 2
McDonald, Joseph 89–90
McDonald, Katherine 81
McDonald, Marguerite 81
McDonald, Mary 81
McDonald, Walter 94
McFarland, Billy 45
McMillan, Duncan 15–16, 18–20,
    23–24
Miller, Eddy 48
Missoula Chamber of Commerce
    81
Missoula County High School
    basketball team 57
Missoula Hamburger Kings inde-
    pendent basketball team 62

Missoula Hereford Association 83
Missoula Mercantile Company 10
modeling 59
Montana Amateur Athletic Union
    90
Montana Board of Athletics 96
Montana Music Rentals 90
Montana School of Mines, Butte,
    basketball team 61
Montana State Chamber of Com-
    merce 65
Montana State College, Bozeman,
    basketball team 60–61
Montana State College, Bozeman,
    football team 5–6, 9, 77–78,
    81
Montana State University, Missou-
    la, basketball team 57–58,
    60, 62–63
Montana State University, Missou-
    la, football team 5–9, 77–81
Morgan, Fred C. (Flathead Agent)
    10, 24
Morin, Lee 46
Mount St. Charles College, Helena
    59–61
Muhammad, Matthew Saad 92
Murphy, Lee Roy 96

N

Neva, George 47–48
Nez Perce Indians 10
Notre Dame University football
    team 34, 74
Noyes, Leonard 77–78

O

O'Day, Sonny 47
Oklahoma Agriculture and Me-
    chanical college football
    team 76

Oklahoma City college football team 78
O'Neill, Jack 15–16, 19–20, 24
Oorange Indians football team 35–38
Oquendo, Angel 92
Oregon State college football team 77–78
Ottawa University football team 73

P

Pablo, Julian 49
Parker, Ray 46
Parlov, Mate 94
Person, Chris 16
Pichette, Marian "Skee" 38
Plains High School basketball team 58
Polson High School basketball team 53–54, 57
Polson Independents baketball team 62–63
Pratt, Henry 33

R

Radick, Nick 47
ranching 81
Red Jacket (Indian chief) 33
Reed, Jimmy 48
Roanoke college football team 76
Rocene, Ray 57–58
rodeos 9–10
Rogers, Leo 95
Ronan Chiefs basketball team 57–58
Ronan High School 90
Ronan High School basketball team 3, 53–59
Roper, Charles 48
Roullier, Caroline Ethier 53
Roullier, Fred 53
Roullier, Lucille Trosper 64–65

Roullier, Phillip "Frenchy" 53–55, 57–65

S

Sacred Heart Society 34–35
St. Benedicts College football team 75
St. Ignatius High School basketball team 54
St. Louis University football team 74
St. Regis High School basketball team 54
St. Xavier College football team 33–34
Sanborn, John 23
San Francisco University football team 77–78
Schaffer, Henry 80
Sedman, Oscar 8, 10
Sharkey, Bill 93
Smith, David 93
Somers independent basketball team 62
stage line 10
Standard Oilers basketball team 63
State Teachers College, Maryville, Mo., football team 73
St. Ignatius Mission boys school 30
Summerhays, Gary 92
Summers, George 76
Superior High School basketball team 54

T

Tacoma Boys' Club, Tacoma, Wash. 90
Tampa University football team 75
Taylor, Eddie 96
Taylor, George 6–7
Temple University football team 74–75

Texas Tech football team 78
Therriault, Henry 10
Thompson Falls High School basketball team 54, 57–58
Thorpe, Jim 2, 35, 37–38, 65
Townsend, Johnny 92
track 31, 34–35, 59
tribal council 38–39, 63, 67, 83
Tulsa University football team 34

U

U.S. Army 49, 65, 77, 81–82
U.S. Indian Claims Commission 67
University of California at Los Angeles football team 77
University of Idaho football team 77–78, 80
University of Idaho, Southern Branch, football team 77
University of North Dakota football team 77–78
University of South Dakota football team 76

V

Van Dorn, Frank 46
VISTA volunteers 83

W

Warfield, Chuck 93
Washburn College football team 74–76

Washington State college football team 77
West, Eden V. 30
Western Montana Independent Basketball Tournament 63
Western Montana Stockmen's Association 81
Wheeler, Marie "Buzzie" 38, 40
Whitefish High School basketball team 57
Whitefish independent basketball team 62
Whitman College basketball team 60–61
Whitmore, Captain 19
Wichita University football team 75
Williamson, Joe 92
Wilson, Ron 93
World Boxing Council 94
World Boxing Council World Cruiserweight Championship 90, 94, 95
wrestling 15–28, 32

X

Xavier University football team 74–76

Y

Yandt, Max 45